YOU WILL BE DUMPED...

YOU WILL BE DUMPED…

You Just Don't Know It Yet!
The Brutal Truth About Relationships
No One Will Tell You and
What To Do Next

SANDRO FERREIRA

Copyright © 2025 by Sandro Ferreira
All rights reserved.

No part of this book may be reproduced, distributed, or transmitted in any form or by any means, including photocopying, recording, or other electronic or mechanical methods, without the prior written permission of the publisher, except in the case of brief quotations embodied in critical reviews and certain other non-commercial uses permitted by copyright law.

Independently Published
ISBN: 978-1-7382060-0-1

AUTHOR'S NOTE

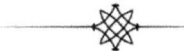

DISCLAIMER: THIS BOOK IS NOT ABOUT ABUSE

This book is written for individuals dealing with standard breakups—relationships that ended due to common challenges like emotional disconnect, misalignment, or personal growth. However, if your relationship involved emotional, physical, verbal, or financial abuse, the strategies in this book may not apply.

Breakups are painful, but no one should ever feel unsafe, manipulated, or controlled. If you experience threats, gaslighting, extreme jealousy, or physical harm in your relationship, healing may require specialized support beyond the steps outlined here.

If you feel unsafe or controlled, please seek outside help. No one should stay in an unhealthy situation out of guilt, fear, or obligation.

You deserve safety.
You deserve respect.
You deserve healing.

DEDICATION

TO ANYONE WHO HAS EVER FELT
THE STING
OF A BROKEN HEART,
THE WEIGHT OF UNSPOKEN WORDS,
OR
THE ACHE OF A LOVE
THAT DIDN'T LAST.
THIS BOOK IS FOR YOU.
MAY IT GUIDE YOU
TO HEALING, STRENGTH,
AND A FUTURE FILLED WITH LOVE—
STARTING WITH YOURSELF..

ACKNOWLEDGMENTS

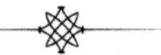

This book would not have been possible without the support of so many people. To my family and friends, thank you for standing by me during the highs and lows of this journey. To my readers, thank you for trusting me to guide you through this process. And finally, to my past self—thank you for surviving the heartbreak that inspired this work.

PREFACE

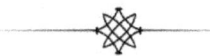

This book was born out of pain, truth, and a desperate desire to understand what went wrong. It was written in the aftermath of a heartbreak I never saw coming, in the wreckage of a relationship I thought would last forever.

For years, I believed my marriage was unshakable. I thought love alone could hold two people together, that commitment meant security, that as long as I worked hard and provided—putting a roof over our heads, food on the table, and financial stability—our relationship would thrive.

But my way of *"loving hard"* wasn't working at all. I was always working, always grinding, always chasing success—thinking that by being a provider, I was being a great partner. Yet, in doing so, I was never truly present. I gave my family everything except me. And by the time I realized it, the foundation I thought was unshakable had already cracked.

I was wrong.

The pain was unlike anything I had ever experienced. One moment, I was living in what I thought was a strong, committed relationship. The next, I was standing in the ruins of something I hadn't even realized was crumbling. I was confused, devastated, and lost in a sea of questions with no answers.

When I look back, I realize that the signs were there—I just didn't want to see them.

Denial is powerful. We tell ourselves stories to make reality easier to bear. We excuse the emotional distance, the missed calls, the fading intimacy. We convince ourselves that things will get better, that it's just a phase, that love will win in the end.

But the truth is, love alone isn't enough.

Relationships don't fall apart overnight—they erode slowly, piece by piece, moment by moment, until one day, there's nothing left to hold on to. And when that moment arrives, the realization is brutal: by the time you notice the ship is sinking, it has already taken on too much water.

This is the book I wish my wife had given me when things started going wrong. If she had handed me these pages, maybe I would have seen what I had been ignoring.

Maybe I would have listened sooner. Maybe I would have made different choices.

Maybe things would have ended differently.

But life doesn't offer do-overs. There is no rewind button. The past is set in stone, but the future is still ours to shape.

I wrote this book because I know I'm not the only one who has been blindsided by the reality of a failing relationship. I know what it feels like to watch someone you love slip away while you stand there, confused and desperate, trying to hold on. I know the feeling of waking up every morning thinking this can't be happening.

And I know the gut-wrenching pain of realizing that it is.

But I also know this: No one should have to go through that alone.

This book will save others who find themselves in the same predicament. It will give you the clarity I wish I had. The subtle shifts, the quiet warnings, the hard truths—these are the things that can save you from heartbreak.

Maybe you're already feeling it—that nagging sense that something is off, even if you can't quite put your finger on it. Maybe you've noticed the growing silence, the way your partner's eyes don't light up when they see you anymore. Maybe you've tried to push these thoughts away, to hold onto hope just a little longer.

I understand. I did the same thing.

But here's what I need you to know:

Ignoring the truth doesn't change it. Avoiding reality doesn't make it any less real. The truth will always come for you—whether you choose to see it or not.

This book isn't about offering false hope or pretending that every relationship can be saved. It's about facing the truth, taking responsibility, and making decisions with clarity and strength. It's about learning to recognize when something is worth fighting for—and when it's already over.

It's about giving you the tools to stop living in denial, to stop waiting for things to magically fix themselves, and to start taking control of your own life.

Because if you don't take control, life will make the choice for you.

If you're looking for validation, for someone to tell you everything will be okay if you just try harder, this isn't that book.

But if you're ready to wake up, to finally see things for what they are, and to take action—whether that means fighting for your relationship or preparing for life after it ends—then this book is for you.

It's time to wake up. It's time to face the truth.

It's time to take action.

With love and tough honesty,

Sandro Ferreira

CONTENTS

Introduction 1

Chapter 1: You Will Be Dumped…The 7 Warning Signs 9

Chapter 2: The Tough Love Wake-Up Call 35

Chapter 3: The Shocking Reality 49

Chapter 4: The Healing Process (Without Toxic Positivity) 61

Chapter 5: Money & Breakups – The Financial Fallout 81

Chapter 6: Men Vs. Women: How We Process Breakups Differently 93

Chapter 7: Rebuilding After It's Over 111

Conclusion: Turning Pain Into Power 125

Resources For Further Healing 139

Additional Resources 141

Final Note 144

About The Author 145

INTRODUCTION

The Hard Truth No One Tells You

Let me ask you something:

Do you think your relationship is safe? When was the last time you and your partner really talked—about dreams, struggles, or even your relationship?

Safe relationships aren't just about avoiding fights; they're about feeling deeply connected.

Does your relationship feel like a place of connection, or are you just coexisting?

Most people assume their relationship is 'safe' until it's too late. But here's the truth: safety comes from effort, not assumptions.

Are you sure your partner is happy?

Happiness is not just about smiling or saying, 'I'm fine.'

Are you paying attention to the little things? The way their tone changes during conversations, their excitement when they talk about your relationship—or the lack of it?

Here's a hard truth: most people don't know when their partner is unhappy because they're too busy focusing on their own needs. When was the last time you really asked—and listened—about how they feel?

Are you paying attention to the subtle signs that they might already be planning to leave?

What are they not saying to you anymore? Have you noticed them avoiding conversations about the future or withdrawing emotionally?

Are they spending more time with others or finding reasons to be away?

People don't wake up one day and decide to leave. They've been deciding for weeks, months, or even years. What signs have you been ignoring?

Every breakup starts with small shifts: less intimacy, shorter conversations, a lack of interest. Are you noticing these signs, or are you in denial?

If you're confident your relationship is unshakable, I challenge you to keep reading. What you'll discover might surprise you—and could save you from heartbreak.

Here's the truth: *one in every two couples* in North America will end their relationship in separation or divorce. It's not just a statistic; it's an epidemic. Even in Christian and Religious circles, where marriage is held as sacred, the numbers are no better.

I know this reality all too well because I'm living it. For years, I thought my relationship was solid.

We attended church in leadership positions and held small prayer groups at our home, had the example of our parent's marriage, but none of that stopped my marriage from unravelling. It felt like I was blindsided when my partner said she wanted a separation. Looking back, the signs were there all along—I just couldn't see them.

You see, most relationships don't die suddenly. They die slowly—through neglect, silence, and denial. And that's exactly why I'm writing this book: to make sure you don't make the same mistakes I did.

What Makes This Book Different

This isn't a *sugar-coated* guide to saving your relationship. I won't waste your time with clichés like *"communication is key"* or *"just pray harder"."* This Book is about facing the truth head-on, taking responsibility, and deciding whether to fight for your relationship or prepare yourself for life after it ends.

If it's not too late, I'll show you how to take bold, decisive steps to prevent your relationship from falling apart.

If it's already too late, I'll guide you on how to heal, rebuild, and come out stronger on the other side.

What will you learn

- ✓ The 7 Signs Your Relationship Is About to End: Subtle but clear red flags most people ignore.
- ✓ Why Tough Love Works: Stop being a victim and start taking control of your life.
- ✓ How to Heal When It's Over: It's OK to cry, but it's not OK to stay stuck.
- ✓ How to Prevent the End, Before is To Late: Practical, no-nonsense steps to rebuild connection and trust.

Who This Book Is For

- ✓ You think your relationship is *"fine"* but haven't felt truly connected to your partner in a while.
- ✓ You've started noticing subtle changes—less affection, shorter conversations—but don't know what to make of it.
- ✓ You've already experienced a breakup or separation and want to prevent it from happening again.
- ✓ You're a Christian who believes in the sanctity of marriage and might be ignoring the signs because divorce feels taboo or unthinkable.
- ✓ You're ready to stop being passive and start being intentional about your relationships.

Why Most People Never See It Coming

Denial is powerful. We tell ourselves stories to avoid facing uncomfortable truths:

"We're just busy right now; things will get better."
"Everyone argues; it doesn't mean anything is wrong."
"If there's a problem, my partner will tell me."

But the truth is that relationships rarely fall apart overnight. They die slowly—through silence, avoidance, and neglect. The signs are always there. Most people are just too distracted or too afraid to see them.

I ignored the signs in my own relationship. I thought everything was fine because I was working hard, providing for my family, and being *"responsible."* But what I didn't realize was that my partner wasn't asking for financial stability or a picture-perfect life—she was asking for connection, attention, and presence. I remember her saying, *"It feels like you love your more than you love me…"* At the time, I dismissed it, thinking, *"I'm doing this for us—she'll understand."*

I didn't understand the gravity of those words until much later. She wasn't asking for grand gestures; she was asking to feel prioritized, seen, and valued. But I was too busy—caught up in the belief that hard work and financial comfort were the ultimate signs of love and commitment.

What I failed to see was that while I was focused on building a comfortable life for my family, I was neglecting the emotional foundation of our relationship. And when the cracks started to form, I convinced myself they were minor, something that could be fixed *"later."* But *"later"* never came.

The Danger of Misaligned Priorities

Many people, especially men, fall into this trap. We think we're being good partners by working hard, paying bills, and providing material stability. But relationships aren't built on achievements—they're built on connection. While you're focused on the next promotion or the next big milestone, your partner may be feeling unseen, unheard, and ultimately unloved.

The warning signs are often subtle: A partner who stops trying to start meaningful conversations; Someone who says, *"It's fine,"* but doesn't look at you the same way.

Less affection, shorter responses, or a growing sense of emotional distance.

We miss these signs because we're too distracted, too comfortable, or too afraid to acknowledge that something might be wrong.

Wake Up Before It's Too Late

The truth is, no amount of financial stability, success, or hard work can make up for a lack of emotional connection. If your partner has stopped *"nagging"* or asking for your attention, that doesn't mean everything is fine—it means they might have already started giving up.

This isn't about blame. It's about awareness. It's about empowering you to take action before it's too late. And if it is too late, it's about helping you rebuild and thrive. You deserve a relationship that works—and a life that thrives whether you're in one or not.

The purpose of this Book is to shake you out of complacency. Don't wait until your partner stops asking for attention. Don't wait until you hear, *"I want a separation."* The time to act is now.

You've already taken the first step by picking up this Book. That means you're willing to face the truth, even if it's uncomfortable. But awareness alone won't save your relationship—or your peace of mind. You need action.

The warning signs are subtle, but they're there. The question is: Will you recognize them before it's too late? Or will you stay stuck in denial until the day your partner says, *"I can't do this anymore"*?

This isn't just about saving your relationship. It's about saving you—your confidence, your clarity, and your ability to thrive no matter what happens. Whether your relationship survives or not, you deserve to walk forward with strength and purpose.

So, let's get started. In the next chapter, we'll dive into the 7 warning signs your partner might be thinking of leaving—and what you can do to spot them before they turn into heartbreak. These signs aren't always obvious, but once you learn to recognize them, you can take steps to address them before it's too late.

"By the time you notice the ship is sinking, it has already taken on too much water."

"Relationships don't fall apart overnight—they erode slowly, piece by piece, moment by moment, until one day, there's nothing left to hold on to."

"Most breakups don't happen when someone leaves. They happen in the silence before—the missed conversations, the avoidance, the emotional withdrawal."

CHAPTER 1
YOU WILL BE DUMPED...
THE 7 WARNING SIGNS

No relationship ends without warning. The problem is that most people fail to notice the signs, either because they're too distracted by daily life or too afraid to confront the possibility that something might be wrong. But here's the truth: relationships don't fall apart overnight. They unravel gradually, often in silence, through a series of subtle shifts that many overlook until it's too late.

Think about this: when was the last time you truly checked in with your partner? Not just a casual *"How was your day?"* but a real conversation about how they're feeling, what they're struggling with, or where they see your relationship heading? If that question makes you uncomfortable or if you can't remember the last time you had such a conversation, it's worth asking yourself why.

Most people live under the assumption that their relationship is the exception. They think, *"Sure, other couples have problems, but we're different."* But statistics tell a different story. Half of all marriages in North America will end in divorce. Even more, relationships that never make it to marriage quietly dissolve. And the most shocking part?

The majority of divorces—around 70%—are initiated by women. That means, for many men, the end of a relationship feels like it comes out of nowhere.

But for women, it's often the result of years of unmet emotional needs, unresolved conflicts, and feeling unseen or unheard.

If you're reading this and thinking, *"This doesn't apply to me,"* I urge you to pause and reflect. Are you absolutely sure your partner isn't quietly unhappy? Do you think you'd recognize the signs if they were? And even if things seem fine on the surface, are you putting in the kind of effort that keeps a relationship alive and thriving?

The truth is, most people believe their relationship is immune to failure until they're confronted with undeniable evidence that it isn't. By the time you're handed divorce papers or hear the words, *"I can't do this anymore,"* the signs have been there for months, if not years. They just went unnoticed—or worse, ignored.

This chapter is your wake-up call. It's an opportunity to look closely at your relationship and ask the hard questions before it's too late. The warning signs we're about to explore are subtle, but they're there. Recognizing them requires courage and self-awareness. It means being willing to admit that something might be wrong and taking responsibility for addressing it. Whether your goal is to save your relationship or prepare yourself for the possibility of its end, understanding these signs is the first step.

Let me be clear: spotting these signs doesn't mean your relationship is doomed. In fact, the earlier you recognize them, the better your chances of turning things around. But ignoring them is a recipe for disaster. Relationships don't thrive on autopilot. They require consistent effort, honest communication, and a willingness to face uncomfortable truths.

As we go through these seven signs, I encourage you to reflect on your own relationship. Be honest with yourself. Have you noticed any of these behaviors in your partner—or in yourself? Are there areas where you've been complacent or blind to the growing cracks in your foundation? These aren't easy questions, but they're necessary ones.

For each sign, we'll explore what it looks like, why it happens, and what you can do about it. You'll also find real-life examples to help you connect these concepts to your own experiences. These stories aren't just hypothetical—they're the realities many couples face. And if you're willing to learn from them, they might just help you avoid becoming another statistic.

One final thing before we dive in: don't let fear hold you back. It's natural to feel uneasy when confronted with the possibility that your relationship might be in trouble.

But ignoring the signs won't make them disappear. On the contrary, avoidance only accelerates the breakdown. By recognizing and addressing these warning signs now, you're giving yourself—and your partner—the chance to create a stronger, healthier, and more fulfilling relationship.

So, let's get started. The seven signs we're about to discuss aren't random—they're patterns observed in countless failing relationships. And while each relationship is unique, these signs tend to show up time and time again. The question is: will you notice them in time?

Sign #1: Emotional Distancing

When someone starts emotionally withdrawing from the relationship, it's one of the clearest signs that something is wrong. Emotional distancing isn't about big fights or dramatic arguments—it's about the absence of connection.

What It Looks Like:
- ✓ Your partner stops sharing their thoughts, feelings, or daily experiences with you.
- ✓ They seem disinterested when you try to connect or initiate conversation.
- ✓ Physical intimacy declines—hugs, kisses, or even sitting close to each other feels forced or absent.

Example:
Jessica and Mike had always been a team. Jessica noticed the first sign of trouble when Mike started spending less time at home. He claimed he was *"working late,"* but even on weekends, he seemed glued to his phone or distracted. Jessica would ask simple questions like, *"How was work today?"* and get responses like, *"Fine,"* or *"The usual."* He stopped telling her about his frustrations or celebrating small wins with her.

When Jessica tried to initiate a conversation about their future, Mike brushed her off with, *"Why are you overthinking this? Everything's fine."* Slowly, Jessica felt like she was living with a stranger.

What to Do:
- ✓ Acknowledge the Distance: Don't brush it off as *"just a phase."* Initiate a conversation to understand what's happening beneath the surface.
- ✓ Rebuild Emotional Intimacy: Schedule uninterrupted time together—no phones, no distractions—and ask open-ended questions about their feelings and thoughts.
- ✓ Seek Honest Feedback: Ask directly if they feel fulfilled in the relationship and listen without defensiveness.

Sign #2: Lack of Future Planning

When your partner stops talking about the future, it's a major red flag. Relationships thrive on shared dreams and goals. If they're no longer including you in their plans, it's a sign they're envisioning a future without you.

What It Looks Like:
- ✓ They avoid conversations about long-term plans, like vacations, finances, or major life goals.
- ✓ They hesitate or show discomfort when you bring up topics like *"Where do you see us in five years?"*
- ✓ They start making independent decisions that exclude you

Example:
David and Sarah used to dream about buying a vacation home near the lake. They'd sit for hours, scrolling through real estate listings and debating which features mattered most. But one day, Sarah stopped engaging in the conversations. When David mentioned a new listing, she changed the subject to her upcoming work project. Soon, Sarah began making solo plans—like applying for a long-term work assignment in another city—without discussing it with David.

When he confronted her, she said, *"I don't know if I see us making those kinds of plans anymore."* David was blindsided, but for Sarah, this was the culmination of months of feeling disconnected.

What to Do:
- ✓ Address the Change: Ask why they've stopped planning together and share how it makes you feel.
- ✓ Revisit Shared Goals: Bring up past dreams you've discussed and explore whether those goals still feel meaningful to them.
- ✓ Evaluate Their Commitment: A lack of future planning often signals a deeper issue. Be prepared to hear difficult truths.

Sign #3: Avoidance of Conflict

Contrary to popular belief, silence is more dangerous than arguing in a relationship. When your partner stops engaging in conflicts, it's often because they no longer see the point—they've emotionally checked out.

What It Looks Like:
- ✓ They avoid difficult conversations or give passive, dismissive responses.
- ✓ Fights that used to feel productive now end with, *"Whatever, it doesn't matter."*
- ✓ They seem uninterested in resolving issues and prefer to *"keep the peace"* rather than address underlying problems.

Example:
Maria and Tom had always been passionate arguers. They'd debate everything, from household chores to future vacation plans, but they always came back together with solutions. Recently, however, Maria noticed that Tom seemed disinterested in resolving even small disagreements. When Maria asked why he wasn't helping around the house, Tom shrugged and said, *"Do whatever you want."* When she brought up financial concerns, he avoided eye contact and responded with, "Why does it matter?"

Maria missed the significance of these moments. Tom's disengagement wasn't apathy—it was a sign he had emotionally checked out.

What to Do:
- ✓ Call Out the Behavior: Share your observations about their avoidance and ask what's behind it.
- ✓ Reframe Conflict as Growth: Remind them that healthy conflict is about strengthening the relationship, not tearing it down.
- ✓ Be Willing to Hear Hard Truths: Their avoidance might stem from feelings of hopelessness about the relationship.

Sign #4: Increased Secrecy or Privacy

When your partner begins to guard their phone, avoid discussing their day, or seem unusually private, it's a potential red flag. Healthy relationships thrive on transparency, but secrecy can indicate emotional withdrawal—or worse, that they're hiding something.

What It Looks Like:
- ✓ They start keeping their phone out of sight or become defensive when you ask about their day.
- ✓ They spend more time on social media or texting but avoid explaining who they're talking to.
- ✓ Their schedule changes and they become vague about their whereabouts or plans.

Example:
Chris and Lisa had a routine—phones on the kitchen counter during dinner and no secrets between them. But over the last few months, Lisa started keeping her phone by her side, even when they were watching TV. Chris noticed she was texting late at night but avoided asking about it, fearing he'd come across as controlling. One evening, Lisa received a call, walked into another room, and whispered for nearly an hour. When Chris asked who it was, she snapped, *"It's none of your business."*

Chris felt uneasy but rationalized her behavior as stress from work. In reality, Lisa was emotionally investing in someone outside the relationship.

What to Do:

✓ Approach Without Accusations: Ask them about the changes you've noticed in a non-confrontational way.

✓ Create Space for Honesty: Let them know you'd rather hear the truth, no matter how difficult, than live in doubt.

✓ Respect Their Privacy, But Set Boundaries: Secrecy erodes trust, and trust is the foundation of any relationship.

Sign #5: Decline in Physical Affection

Physical intimacy is one of the clearest indicators of emotional connection in a relationship. When affection fades, it's often a sign that deeper emotional issues are at play.

What It Looks Like:
- ✓ They no longer initiate hugs, kisses, or other forms of touch.
- ✓ Physical intimacy feels mechanical or like an obligation.
- ✓ They seem uncomfortable or disinterested when you try to be affectionate.

Example:
Jake and Emily had always been a physically affectionate couple. They'd kiss before work, hold hands on walks, and snuggle while watching movies. Over time, Jake noticed Emily pulling away. She'd turn her head during goodnight kisses and say, "I'm just tired." When Jake reached out to hold her hand, Emily would gently move away, claiming she needed to focus on something else. Jake thought she was stressed from her new job, but the truth was deeper—Emily no longer felt emotionally connected to him, and it was showing in her body language.

What to Do:
- ✓ Address the Shift: Talk openly about how the lack of physical connection makes you feel.
- ✓ Work on Emotional Intimacy First: Physical affection often follows emotional closeness, so start by rebuilding trust and emotional connection.
- ✓ Be Patient but Persistent: Don't push, but don't ignore the issue either—it's a symptom of a larger problem.

Sign #6: Disinterest in Shared Activities

When your partner stops engaging in the activities you once enjoyed together, it's often a sign they're losing interest in the relationship as a whole. Shared experiences are the glue of a relationship, and their absence creates emotional distance.

What It Looks Like:
- ✓ They no longer join you for date nights, hobbies, or other activities you used to enjoy together.
- ✓ They seem distracted or disinterested when spending time with you.
- ✓ They prioritize time with friends, work, or solo activities over shared moments.

Example:
Amanda and Ryan loved hiking. Every Saturday, they'd lace up their boots, pack snacks, and head to the nearest trail. But lately, Ryan started making excuses not to go. He'd say, I or *"I'm not feeling up for it."* When Amanda suggested switching to a shorter trail, Ryan responded, *"Why don't you go without me?"* At first, Amanda believed him, but she soon noticed a pattern: Ryan was prioritizing time with his friends and spending more hours at the gym, alone. Amanda realized that the activities that once bonded them had become an afterthought for Ryan.

What to Do:

- ✓ Rekindle Shared Interests: Suggest activities you both used to enjoy and see if they're willing to participate. Address Their Absence: Let them know how much those moments mean to you and ask why they've pulled away. Evaluate the Bigger Picture: If disinterest persists, it could signal deeper emotional detachment.

Sign #7: A General Feeling That Something Is Off

Sometimes, the most telling sign isn't a specific behavior but a gut feeling. You might sense a shift in their energy, a lack of warmth, or an unspoken tension that wasn't there before. This intuition is often your subconscious picking up on subtle cues.

What It Looks Like:
- ✓ Conversations feel strained or surface-level.
- ✓ You notice subtle changes in their tone, body language, or attitude.
- ✓ You feel uneasy, like you're walking on eggshells or something is being left unsaid.

Example:
Carla couldn't put her finger on it, but something about her husband Mark felt different. He wasn't overtly rude or distant, but the warmth in his voice was gone. When she asked about his day, he answered politely but without enthusiasm. Conversations that used to flow naturally now felt awkward and forced. At family gatherings, Mark seemed disengaged, often scrolling on his phone instead of interacting with their relatives. One evening, as they sat silently at the dinner table, Carla blurted out, *"Are you okay?*

You seem distant lately." Mark's response was vague: *"I'm fine, just tired."* Carla knew there was more to the story, but Mark wasn't ready to share it.

What to Do:
- ✓ Trust Your Intuition: Don't dismiss the feeling that something is off—dig deeper.
- ✓ Have an Honest Conversation: Share your observations and ask if there's something they haven't been saying.
- ✓ Be Prepared for the Truth: Sometimes, your gut is right, and you need to be ready to face the reality of the situation.

Recognizing the Signs

The 7 signs are your wake-up call. They're not definitive proof that your relationship will end, but they're indicators that something is seriously wrong. The question is, what will you do now that you've seen them?

Discussion Questions:

1. Which of the seven warning signs have you noticed in your own relationship?
2. Have you ever ignored red flags in the past? If so, what made you overlook them?
3. How do you typically respond when you sense distance in a relationship—do you address it directly or withdraw?
4. If your partner has emotionally checked out, do you believe the relationship can still be saved? Why or why not?
5. How does your pride or fear play a role in your ability to recognize problems early?
6. If your best friend described a relationship that mirrors yours, what advice would you give them?
7. What is one action step you can take this week to improve communication and connection with your partner?

"You can be a victim or you can take control—but you can't do both."

"Ignoring the truth doesn't change it. Avoiding reality doesn't make it any less real. The truth will always come for you—whether you choose to see it or not."

"If you want to save your relationship, stop asking why they are leaving and start asking why they don't want to stay."

CHAPTER 2
THE TOUGH LOVE WAKE-UP CALL

The Reality Check

Let's face it: blaming your partner is easy. It feels good at the moment because it absolves you of responsibility. You can point to all the things they didn't do, the ways they hurt you, and the times they let you down. But here's the truth: if you're reading this book, you're probably not happy with where your relationship is—and that means it's time to take a hard look in the mirror.

No relationship falls apart because of just one person. Even if your partner is the one pulling away, there are actions you've taken—or haven't taken—that have contributed to where you are today. Acknowledging that isn't about blaming yourself; it's about empowering yourself to create change. If you don't, you'll keep repeating the same patterns, whether it's in this relationship or the next.

This chapter isn't for the faint of heart. It's going to challenge you. It's going to ask you to confront truths you've been avoiding. But if you're serious about saving your relationship—or even just saving yourself—then tough love is where it starts.

The Problem with Playing the Victim

When your relationship starts to unravel, playing the victim feels natural. *"I did everything I could, and they still left."* I While these feelings are valid, staying in this mindset only hurts you more.

What Playing the Victim Does to You

It Keeps You Stuck: When you see yourself as the victim, you're waiting for someone else to fix the problem. You're giving away your power to create change.

It Destroys Your Confidence: Constantly blaming others reinforces the belief that you're helpless. Over time, this erodes your self-esteem and makes you feel like you're not in control of your own life.

It Sabotages Growth: Relationships are mirrors. They reflect our strengths and weaknesses. By refusing to own your role in the relationship, you miss the opportunity to learn and grow.

What Playing the Victim Looks Like:
Blaming Without Reflecting

Example: Sarah constantly blamed her partner, Greg, for their financial struggles.

She would say things like, *"You're the one who spends too much on unnecessary things!"* Yet, Sarah never looked at her own habits of impulse shopping or failure to stick to a budget. Her refusal to reflect on her role in the issue prevented them from solving their financial problems together.

Actionable Step: Instead of pointing fingers, Sarah could track her own spending for a month and discuss budgeting solutions with Greg as a team.

Dwelling on Past Wrongs:

Example: After Jake forgot their anniversary, his wife, Emily, brought it up during every argument for the next six months. Jake began withdrawing emotionally, feeling like he could never move past his mistake.

Actionable Step: Emily could set a boundary for addressing past mistakes: discuss the hurt openly, seek resolution, and agree not to revisit it unless it directly relates to current behavior.

Waiting for the Other Person to Change:

Example: Paul felt distant from his partner, Lily, and kept saying,

"I'll make an effort when she does." This stalemate only deepened the divide between them.

Actionable Step: Paul could focus on what he can control by initiating small acts of kindness, like preparing Lily's favorite meal or writing her a thoughtful note. These actions can inspire change without waiting for reciprocity.

Example: Alex and Laura had been married for 10 years. When Laura asked for a separation, Alex was devastated. He told his friends, *"I worked so hard to give her a good life, and this is how she thanks me?"* For weeks, Alex replayed every moment he felt unappreciated. But what he failed to see was how often Laura had tried to connect with him and how many times he'd dismissed her concerns with, *"I don't have time for this."* Laura didn't leave because Alex worked hard; she left because he made her feel invisible.

The Hard Truth About Relationships

Here's a fact no one likes to admit: love isn't enough to sustain a relationship. It takes consistent effort, humility, and the willingness to grow together. If you're not putting in the work, you're letting the relationship stagnate—and stagnation leads to decay.

Why Relationships Fail:

Unmet Emotional Needs: Most people don't leave because of one catastrophic event. They leave because of a thousand small moments where they felt unseen or unsupported.

Example: Maria and David stopped communicating openly after having kids. Maria felt overwhelmed by childcare, while David focused solely on work. Maria started saying, *"You never listen to me,"* and David felt attacked. The truth was, both of them had unmet emotional needs—they just expressed them in different ways.

Actionable Step: Schedule weekly check-ins where both partners share one thing they need emotionally that week. For Maria, it might be *"an hour to myself."* For David, it might be *"words of appreciation for my hard work."*

Lack of Accountability: When one or both partners refuse to own their mistakes, resentment builds, creating an emotional wall.

Example: When conflicts arose, Rachel always blamed her partner, Mark, for being *"too sensitive."* This dismissiveness made Mark feel invalidated, and over time, he stopped expressing his feelings altogether. Rachel didn't realize her defensiveness was eroding trust.

Actionable Step: Rachel could practice pausing during arguments to ask, "What's my role in this conflict?" This self-reflection creates space for constructive dialogue instead of blame.

Complacency: Over time, people stop putting in the same effort they did in the beginning. This leads to a gradual disconnect that's hard to repair.

Example: Mike and Emma were the couple everyone admired. They had been together for 15 years and seemed inseparable. But over time, Mike stopped doing the little things that made Emma feel loved—no more date nights, no random texts to say *"I'm thinking of you."* Emma tried to address it, but Mike brushed her off, saying, *"You know I love you, right?"* What Mike didn't realize was that Emma needed more than words—she needed effort. When she eventually left, Mike was stunned, but the truth was, the warning signs had been there for years.

Actionable Step: Jason could reignite effort by revisiting one of their favorite shared activities, like recreating their first date or planning a surprise outing. Consistency is key—small actions over time rebuild the connection.

Questions to Ask Yourself:
Have I been showing up for my partner emotionally, or have I been coasting on autopilot?

Am I quick to blame them for problems, or do I take time to reflect on my role?

Have I allowed myself to become complacent, assuming my partner will always be there no matter what?

Taking Responsibility Without Blame
Taking responsibility doesn't mean taking all the blame. It means owning your role in the relationship while recognizing that your partner has their own accountability too. It's about shifting from *"Why is this happening to me?"* to *"What can I do to make things better?"*

How to Take Responsibility:
Reflect Honestly: Take time to identify the ways you've contributed to the relationship's struggles. This might mean acknowledging moments of neglect, poor communication, or defensiveness.

Have Open Conversations: Share your reflections with your partner in a way that invites dialogue, not blame. For example: *"I realize I haven't been as attentive to your needs as I should have been. I want to change that. Can we talk about how we can move forward together?"*

Commit to Action: Words mean nothing without follow-through. Whether it's scheduling regular quality time, being more present, or addressing conflicts head-on, consistency is key.

Example: After months of reflection, Alex realized he had been emotionally absent in his marriage. Instead of wallowing in guilt, he decided to take action. He apologized to Laura, not to win her back, but to take ownership of his mistakes. He said, *"I see now that I wasn't there for you the way I should have been. I'm sorry for the ways I made you feel invisible. I'm working on being a better person, whether or not we stay together."* This honesty and accountability didn't guarantee reconciliation, but it gave Alex the clarity and confidence to move forward.

When Stopping the Victim Mindset Is Too Late
Sometimes, no matter how much effort you put into shifting your mindset, the relationship is already too far gone. Your partner might have emotionally checked out, moved on, or decided that reconciliation isn't possible. While this is a painful reality, it's also an opportunity to reclaim your power and focus on rebuilding yourself.

Signs It's Too Late to Repair the Relationship:
Your Partner Has Clearly Communicated It's Over:
If they've explicitly stated they no longer see a future with you and are firm in their decision, it's important to respect their boundaries.

Example: Mark's wife, Sarah, told him, *"I've been unhappy for years, and I don't think we can fix this."* Though Mark tried to apologize and make amends, Sarah had already mentally and emotionally moved on.

They've Taken Steps Toward Separation:
Actions like moving out, filing for divorce, or cutting off communication are strong indicators that they're no longer invested in repairing the relationship.

Example: When Maria's husband filed for divorce after months of emotional distance, she realized that trying to *"win him back"* was only prolonging her own healing.

There's No Willingness to Engage:
If your partner refuses therapy, conversations, or any attempt to reconnect, it's a sign they've given up on the relationship.

Digital Detox:
Stop Letting Social Media Reopen the Wound. One of the biggest mistakes people make after a breakup is keeping digital ties to their ex.

Even if you've cut off direct contact, social media keeps the breakup alive in your mind. Seeing them happy, dating, or moving on (even if it's fake) prevents healing.

If you're serious about moving forward, you must take control of your online space. Mute, Unfollow, or Block!

Ask yourself:
- ✓ Do you check their Social media more than once a day?
- ✓ Do you find yourself analyzing their posts, wondering if they're about you?
- ✓ Does seeing their face, name, or status updates ruin your mood?

If yes to any of the above, it's time to mute, unfollow, or block—at least temporarily.

Mute – If you don't want to block them but need space, mute their posts/stories.

Unfollow – If seeing their updates triggers emotions, remove them from your feed.

Block – If you keep checking their page out of habit, a full block might be necessary.

Truth Bomb: You don't need to prove *"you're mature"* by keeping them on your social media. Prioritize your healing over appearances.

The "No Lurking" Rule
Do not stalk their page.
Do not check their tagged photos.
Do not analyze their Spotify playlist updates.

If you have the urge to check, remind yourself:

What will this do for me? Will it help me move forward or keep me stuck?

Would I want them checking on me? If the answer is no, then don't do it.

🪔 *Pro Tip: If you keep falling into the trap, log out of social media for at least a week or use a website blocker to remove temptation.*

Managing Mutual Friends

Breakups don't just separate two people—they can divide friend groups, too.

You might have mutual friends who still talk to your ex, and whether they mean to or not, they might keep you updated on their life.

Set Boundaries with Mutual Friends:

Tell them upfront – *"I don't want to hear about my ex right now. No updates, no stories, no 'you won't believe what they did' texts."*

- ✓ Avoid hanging out in spaces where your ex will be.
- ✓ If a friend keeps bringing them up, distance yourself for a while.

This isn't about *"being petty"*—it's about protecting your peace.

Your healing is more important than knowing what your ex is doing. Focus on YOUR next chapter, not theirs.

Why Stopping the Victim Mindset Still Matters

Even if the relationship can't be saved, shifting out of the victim mindset is crucial for your personal growth and future happiness. Holding onto blame, resentment, or regret will only weigh you down and prevent you from moving forward.

Reclaim Your Power:

When you stop seeing yourself as a victim, you take control of your life. You can't change the past, but you can choose how you respond to it.

Example: Instead of blaming his ex for leaving, John decided to focus on improving himself. He started therapy, reconnected with friends, and explored hobbies he'd neglected during the relationship.

Break the Cycle:
Without reflection and accountability, you risk repeating the same patterns in future relationships.

Example: Lisa recognized that her tendency to shut down during conflicts contributed to her breakup. By working on her communication skills, she entered her next relationship with healthier habits.

Build a Stronger You:
Shifting your focus from saving the relationship to saving yourself allows you to heal, grow, and rediscover your identity.

Example: After her divorce, Emily joined a support group for single parents and enrolled in a personal development course. These steps helped her rebuild her confidence and find purpose beyond her role as a partner.

Actionable Steps When It's Too Late:
Accept the Reality:
Acknowledge that the relationship has ended and resist the urge to dwell on "what ifs." Acceptance doesn't mean giving up—it means freeing yourself to focus on what's next.

Forgive Yourself and Your Partner:
Holding onto anger or guilt will only prolong your pain. Forgiveness is a gift you give yourself to let go and move on.

Set New Goals:
Shift your energy toward personal growth. Whether it's improving your health, advancing your career, or deepening your faith, setting goals will help you find direction and purpose.

Surround Yourself with Support:
Lean on friends, family, or a therapist to navigate the emotional challenges of separation. Isolation will only make the process harder.

Reflect and Learn:
Journal about what the relationship taught you—both the good and the bad. Use these lessons to build healthier connections in the future.

Case Study: Learning to Let Go

Sophia had been in a relationship with Matt for eight years when he told her he wanted to end things. At first, Sophia begged him to reconsider, pointing out all the ways she was willing to change. But Matt had already made up his mind. For months, Sophia clung to the hope that he might come back, even after he started dating someone new.

One day, a friend told Sophia, *"You can't make someone love you. But you can love yourself enough to let them go."* That conversation changed everything. Sophia began focusing on herself—joining a fitness class, reconnecting with her faith, and building a new social circle. While the pain of losing Matt didn't disappear overnight, Sophia found strength and clarity in letting go.

Tough Love Reminder: Moving Forward Isn't Failure

If the relationship ends, it doesn't mean you've failed. It means you're entering a new chapter. By stopping the victim mindset, you're setting yourself up for a future filled with growth, self-discovery, and healthier connections.

Discussion Questions:

1. What was your biggest *"wake-up call"* while reading this chapter?
2. In what ways have you avoided facing the truth in your relationship?
3. If you had to be brutally honest with yourself, what is the biggest mistake you've made in your relationship?
4. Have you been prioritizing comfort over clarity, staying in a relationship that might already be over?
5. If your partner gave you a raw, unfiltered truth about how they feel, what do you think they would say?
6. Imagine your relationship ended today—what is one thing you would regret not doing or saying?
7. What immediate change can you make in the way you show up in your relationship?

"Most people don't know when their partner is unhappy because they're too busy focusing on their own needs."

"People don't wake up one day and decide to leave. They've been deciding for weeks, months, or even years."

"The moment they stop arguing, stop asking for attention, and stop trying—it's already over."

CHAPTER 3

THE SHOCKING REALITY

Let's start with a fact most people don't want to hear: Relationships are failing at an alarming rate. The numbers aren't just shocking—they're heartbreaking.

The Numbers Don't Lie

In North America, 50% of marriages end in divorce. That's one out of every two couples standing at the altar, believing their love will last forever, only to watch it unravel.

70% of divorces are initiated by women. That means in most cases, it's the wife who decides the relationship is no longer worth fighting for.

Only 25% of separated couples ever reconcile. The other 75% move on, often carrying emotional baggage that affects future relationships.

And these statistics don't even account for long-term, unmarried relationships that quietly fall apart. Breakups don't just happen in courtrooms—they happen in homes, apartments, and text messages every single day.

Divorce Rates in the U.S.: According to the National Center for Health Statistics, the divorce rate in the U.S. was 2.4 per 1,000 population in 2022, down from 4.0 per 1,000 in 2000. – Forbes

Divorce Rates in Canada: Statistics Canada reported that the annual divorce rate declined from about 10 divorces per 1,000 married women in the early 2000s to 6 divorces per 1,000 married women in 2016. – Vanier Institute

Divorce Initiation by Women: A study published in the American Sociological Review found that approximately 70% of divorces are initiated by women.

Why These Numbers Matter
These statistics aren't just abstract figures—they represent real lives, real heartbreak, and real consequences. They paint a picture of how fragile relationships can be when we fail to nurture them.

What these numbers reveal is that no relationship is immune to failure.

It doesn't matter how long you've been together, how much you love each other, or how strong your foundation seems. Relationships don't end because of one big blowout; they unravel over time—through small, seemingly insignificant cracks that go unnoticed.

When you see that 70% of divorces are initiated by women, the message is clear: there's a disconnect happening in relationships that men often fail to recognize. Women aren't leaving because they want to; they're leaving because they feel unheard, unsupported, and emotionally detached. For every relationship that ends in separation, there's a story of missed opportunities, ignored warnings, and silent pleas for connection.

Here's why this matters to you:
Are you paying attention to your partner's needs, or are you assuming everything is fine?

Do you notice when they pull away emotionally, or are you too focused on external distractions?

Most importantly, do you know how to fix what's broken—or are you hoping it will resolve itself?

These numbers matter because they serve as a wake-up call.

If you're reading this, you still have time to act. You have the chance to confront the reality of your relationship, address the cracks, and rebuild before it's too late. But that requires honesty, effort, and a willingness to see what you might have been ignoring. It's a statistic that shocks many men: women initiate 70% of divorces. While some might jump to conclusions or oversimplify the reasons, the reality is nuanced and deeply rooted in unmet emotional, physical, and relational needs. Understanding these factors is not about blame—it's about awareness, growth, and creating healthier relationships in the future.

For many women, emotional connection is the foundation of a relationship. When this connection erodes, the relationship begins to feel hollow, leading to dissatisfaction and eventual separation.

Sexual Dissatisfaction
Physical intimacy is often a barometer of a relationship's overall health. For many women, sexual dissatisfaction stems not just from physical incompatibility but also from a lack of emotional connection or effort in the bedroom.

Common Causes of Sexual Dissatisfaction:
- ✓ Lack of effort or creativity in maintaining intimacy.
- ✓ Feeling unattractive or unappreciated by their partner.
- ✓ Persistent issues like mismatched libidos or ignoring expressed desires.

Impact on the Relationship:
Over time, unaddressed sexual dissatisfaction leads to feelings of rejection, frustration, or even resentment, which can create an insurmountable divide.

Physical intimacy is a two-way street. Open communication and willingness to adapt are critical for maintaining a healthy connection.

Financial Stress
Finances are one of the top causes of marital tension and divorce. For many women, financial instability or disagreements about money management create feelings of insecurity and stress that eventually become unbearable.

Examples of Financial Stress:
Disagreements over spending, saving, or budgeting.

A partner's refusal to take responsibility for financial planning; Unequal contributions, where one partner carries the financial burden while the other is perceived as disengaged.

Why It Matters:
Financial stress isn't just about money—it's about trust, partnership, and shared goals. If these elements are missing, the relationship starts to crumble. Financial health is a team effort. Transparency, planning, and shared responsibility are non-negotiable.

Infidelity and Betrayal

Few things break trust as irreparably as infidelity. Whether it's physical cheating, emotional affairs, or repeated betrayals, these actions undermine the foundation of any relationship.

Why Women Leave After Infidelity:
Trust, once broken, is incredibly difficult to rebuild.

Betrayal often magnifies existing issues in the relationship, such as emotional neglect or unmet needs.

Many women view infidelity as a clear indicator that the relationship no longer holds the respect or commitment it once did. Trust is the backbone of any relationship. Without it, the relationship cannot survive.

Inequality in the Partnership

Women often carry a disproportionate share of the emotional and physical labor in a relationship, from managing household chores to navigating family dynamics. When this imbalance goes unaddressed, resentment builds.

Examples of Inequality:

A partner who doesn't contribute equally to household responsibilities.

Expectation for one partner (often the woman) to handle emotional support, child-rearing, and logistics alone.

Dismissing or downplaying the mental load carried by the other partner.

Impact: Over time, this imbalance creates feelings of being unsupported, undervalued, and overwhelmed, leading many women to reevaluate the relationship.

A partnership thrives when both individuals share the load equally, not when one person is carrying the weight alone.

Lack of Growth or Compatibility
People grow and evolve over time, but not always in the same direction. When partners stop aligning on core values, goals, or lifestyles, it can create an irreparable divide.

Examples of Divergence:

Differing views on major life decisions, such as having children, career priorities, or lifestyle choices.

One partner growing emotionally, intellectually, or spiritually while the other remains stagnant.

Many women leave not because they dislike their partner, but because they feel the relationship is holding them back from personal growth or fulfillment. Growth is essential for both individuals and the relationship. Stagnation is often the beginning of the end.

Emotional or Physical Abuse
Abuse, whether physical, emotional, or verbal, is one of the most painful and undeniable reasons women initiate divorce. For many, the decision to leave is an act of survival and self-preservation.

Examples of Abuse:
- ✓ Constant criticism, manipulation, or gaslighting.
- ✓ Controlling behaviors that limit independence or self-expression.
- ✓ Physical violence or threats.

Safety and well-being become the priority, and staying in the relationship is no longer an option.

No one deserves to endure abuse in any form. Recognizing the signs and prioritizing safety is critical.

Understanding the Patterns
The reasons women initiate divorce are often interconnected. For instance, financial stress can lead to emotional disconnect, which might magnify dissatisfaction in other areas like intimacy or trust. Recognizing these patterns is crucial for personal growth and future relationships.

If you find yourself blindsided by your partner's decision to leave, it's important to step back and reflect honestly.

Ask yourself:
- ✓ Have I been actively listening to their needs, or have I been dismissing them?
- ✓ Have I taken responsibility for my share of the emotional, financial, or physical labor?
- ✓ Have I been growing with them, or have I become complacent?

Understanding these factors isn't just about saving the relationship—it's about becoming a better partner and individual, now and in the future.

Why Men Often Miss the Signs

Many men, *myself included*, have been conditioned to equate providing and hard work with being a good partner. We believe that by ensuring financial stability and comfort, we're fulfilling our role. While these efforts are important, they can sometimes lead us to overlook the emotional needs of our partners.

In my own experience, I was so focused on working hard to provide a comfortable life for my family that I missed the subtle cues my partner was giving me. She would say things like, *"The day I stop asking for attention will be too late,"* and *"Please pick me."* At the time, I dismissed these comments, thinking my dedication to work was enough. I failed to see that she was expressing a deep need for emotional connection and presence.

This is a common scenario. Men may misinterpret or overlook their partner's appeals for attention, affection, or communication, especially when preoccupied with external responsibilities. By the time the signs become undeniable, the relationship may have already suffered significant damage.

The Danger of Complacency

If you're a man reading this, you might be thinking, *"But I'm working hard to provide for my family. Isn't that enough?"* I get it—I was in the same mindset. I believed my hard work and sacrifices would naturally translate into love and appreciation. But relationships don't work that way.

While I was busy focusing on external success, my partner was quietly pulling away.

She was asking for attention in subtle ways—ways I didn't recognize because I thought I was already doing enough. When she stopped asking, I thought we had reached a place of comfort. In reality, she had reached a place of indifference.

The Uncomfortable Truth

Breakups and divorces don't happen overnight. They build over months or even years of unresolved tension, unmet needs, and growing emotional distance. The signs are always there—less eye contact, fewer shared laughs, a growing sense of being *"roommates"* instead of partners.

Most people miss these signs because they're too focused on what's happening outside the relationship. Work, kids, finances, and even church commitments can blind us to what's happening right in front of us. By the time we realize what's wrong, it's often too late.

Discussion Questions:

1. What truth in this chapter hit you the hardest? Why?
2. Have you ever been in a relationship where the other person moved on faster than you expected? How did that impact you?
3. How do you typically process loss and rejection—do you shut down, seek distractions, or confront it head-on?
4. If closure isn't guaranteed, how can you create it for yourself?
5. What is one belief about love or relationships that this chapter made you question?
6. Looking back, were there moments where you felt your partner was already preparing to leave, but you ignored it?
7. How can you start focusing on yourself instead of waiting for answers from someone who has already left?

'You can be a victim

or

you can take control

—but you can't do both.'

"Love is not a strategy. It's an emotion. And emotions alone don't build lasting relationships."

"The problem isn't that they don't love you—it's that they don't feel loved by you."

"A healthy relationship is built with effort, intention, and action—not just feelings."

CHAPTER 4
THE HEALING PROCESS (WITHOUT TOXIC POSITIVITY)

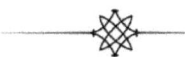

Introduction: Accepting the End

Breakups hurt. There's no sugarcoating it. Whether it ended with a long, drawn-out decline or a sudden, gut-wrenching moment, the pain of losing a relationship can feel unbearable. They leave you feeling raw, exposed, and vulnerable. It doesn't matter if you saw it coming or if it blindsided you—it still feels like your world has been turned upside down. But here's the truth: the pain is part of the process. It's not something to be avoided or suppressed—it's something to confront and work through. Healing starts with accepting the pain. Ignoring it, numbing it, or pretending it doesn't exist won't make it go away. The only way out is through.

For many people, especially in Christians and Religious circles, the end of a relationship carries a unique burden. You might feel like you've failed God, your partner, or yourself. You might wonder if you're breaking sacred vows or giving up on something you were meant to fight for. But here's the reality: not all relationships are meant to last, and that's OK. Accepting this truth is the first step to healing.

It's OK to cry. It's OK to feel angry, lost, or even relieved. But what's not OK is staying stuck in those emotions. This chapter is about working through the pain with honesty, faith, and action.

Healing isn't about waiting for time to pass—it's about taking deliberate steps to rebuild yourself. Cry if you need to. Scream if it helps. But whatever you do, don't let this pain break you. Let it build you.

The Tough Love Truth About Breakups

Here's the hard truth: your relationship ended for a reason. Whether it was incompatibility, unmet needs, or a loss of connection, something wasn't working, and ignoring that reality will only prolong your pain. Too often, people romanticize their ex or hold onto an idealized version of the relationship, convincing themselves it was perfect despite the cracks that were clearly there.

Let's get one thing straight: a breakup doesn't define you. It's a moment in your life, not the totality of who you are. But for many people, especially those who value long-term commitment, a breakup feels like failure. In Christian and religious circles, this feeling is amplified by the stigma surrounding separation and divorce. The shame, the judgment, and the whispers behind closed doors can make you feel like you've let everyone down.

Why the Pain Feels So Intense

You're Mourning a Dream: Breakups aren't just about losing a person; they're about losing the future you imagined with them.

Your Identity Feels Shaken: If you've built your sense of self around the relationship, its end can leave you feeling unmoored.

You're Facing the Unknown: The fear of being alone or starting over can be paralyzing, especially if you've been in the relationship for a long time.

The Hard Reality:
It's Not Just About You:
A breakup often feels deeply personal, but relationships are a partnership. Your ex's decision to leave says as much about them as it does about you.

Example: James struggled with feelings of failure after his wife left him. He thought, *"If I had been better, she would've stayed."* But the truth was, his wife had been dealing with her own unresolved issues that James couldn't fix for her.

You're Not Alone: It's easy to believe you're the only one going through this pain, but the reality is, millions of people experience breakups every year.

The difference between those who move on and those who stay stuck is their ability to face the pain and rebuild.

Breakups Aren't Always *"Bad"*:

While painful, a breakup can also be a chance to let go of something that wasn't working and create space for something better.

Tough Love Reminder: Sometimes, the breakup is the blessing you don't recognize yet.

Let Yourself Feel It—But Don't Stay There.

Crying isn't a sign of weakness; it's a release. Bottling up your emotions will only lead to resentment, anger, or bitterness. But here's the key: while it's important to let yourself feel the pain, you can't let it define you.

What Feeling the Pain Looks Like:

Allowing yourself moments to grieve without judgment.

Journaling your emotions to gain clarity on what you're experiencing. Talking to a trusted friend or therapist who can offer support without enabling self-pity.

What Staying in the Pain Looks Like:

- ✓ Replaying every detail of the breakup obsessively.
- ✓ Blaming yourself—or your ex—without seeking understanding.
- ✓ Avoiding healthy coping mechanisms like exercise, prayer, or social interaction.

Challenging the Taboos

In many religious circles, breakups, separations, and divorces are seen as taboo. The pressure to stay in a relationship at all costs can make you feel trapped, even when it's clear the relationship is toxic or irreparable. But staying for appearances or out of fear of judgment isn't the answer.

What Society Gets Wrong: -Perfectionism Is a Lie

No one's relationship is perfect, and pretending yours is only adds unnecessary pressure.

Tough Love Reminder: God—or whatever higher purpose you believe in—doesn't ask for perfection. What's asked of you is honesty, accountability, and growth.

Sacrifice Without Reciprocity Isn't Noble.

Many people are taught that enduring hardship in a relationship is a sign of strength or faith. But sacrifice without mutual effort or respect is not noble—it's self-neglect.

Example: Claire stayed in her marriage for years, believing it was her duty to *"fix"* her husband's behavior. In the end, she realized she was enabling his bad habits, and leaving was the first step toward their healing.

You're Not Defined by Your Relationship Status:

Whether single, married, separated, or divorced, your worth isn't tied to your relationship status. Your value comes from who you are, not who you're with.

Embracing the Pain

The hardest part of a breakup is facing the emotions head-on. It's tempting to distract yourself, stay busy, or bury the feelings under work, hobbies, or even new relationships. But healing doesn't happen without acknowledging the pain.

The Pain of Breakups:

Breakups aren't just painful—they're life-altering. They leave you questioning your worth, your decisions, and sometimes even your future. The pain of a breakup isn't confined to the heart; it seeps into every aspect of your life. It's the hollow feeling in your chest when you wake up in the morning and realize they're not there. It's the way the silence in your home seems louder than it ever has. It's the endless stream of "what-ifs" and *"if-onlys"* running through your mind.

But here's the thing: pain, as unbearable as it feels, is also a teacher. It reveals what matters most to you, what you need to heal, and what you're capable of overcoming.

The Many Layers of Breakup Pain
The Loss of Routine:

When you're in a relationship, your partner becomes a part of your daily rhythm. The good morning texts, the shared meals, the inside jokes—they're woven into the fabric of your life. A breakup rips those threads apart, leaving you with a void that feels impossible to fill.

Example: Sarah used to call her partner every day on her lunch break. After their breakup, lunchtime became unbearable. She found herself scrolling through old messages, clinging to the routine she had lost.

The Identity Crisis:

Relationships shape who we are. When they end, it's like losing a part of yourself. You might think, *"Who am I without them?"* or *"What do I even like to do anymore?"* The pain isn't just about missing them—it's about rediscovering who you are without them.

Tough Love Reminder: This is an opportunity to rebuild your identity on your terms.

The Weight of Regret:

Breakups often leave you replaying every fight, every decision, and every missed opportunity. The *"what-ifs"* can feel like they're eating you alive.

Example: Jake couldn't stop thinking about the last argument he had with his ex. He thought, *"If I had just kept my mouth shut, maybe she wouldn't have left."* But the truth is, breakups are rarely about one single moment.

The Fear of the Unknown:
A breakup is a disruption of the life you imagined. You might wonder, *"What now?"* or *"Will I ever find someone else?"* This uncertainty can be paralyzing, making the pain feel even heavier.

Tough Love Reminder: The unknown is scary, but it's also a blank canvas waiting for you to create something new.

Why the Pain Feels Overwhelming
Breakups Mimic Grief:
Losing a relationship is like experiencing a death. You're grieving the loss of a connection, a shared future, and sometimes even a version of yourself. Grief is messy—it doesn't follow a straight line. Some days, you'll feel like you're moving forward, and other days, it will hit you like a tidal wave.

The Loneliness is Crushing:
Even if you have friends or family to lean on, breakups can make you feel isolated. You might think, *"No one understands what I'm going through."* This loneliness amplifies the pain, making it harder to see a way out.

Example: Claire surrounded herself with supportive friends after her divorce, but she still felt a deep loneliness when she came home to an empty house. It wasn't just the absence of her partner—it was the absence of a shared life.

Societal Stigma:
In Christians and religious circles, breakups and divorces carry an additional layer of shame. You might feel judged by your community

or worry about how others perceive you. This external pressure can make the internal pain even harder to bear.

Your worth isn't defined by what others think of you. The people who truly matter will support you, not judge you.

What Pain Teaches You

While it might not feel like it now, the pain of a breakup has something to offer. It's a wake-up call—a chance to confront your vulnerabilities, reassess your priorities, and rebuild stronger than before.

It Shows You What You Need:

Pain often reveals the gaps in your life or relationship that need to be addressed. Maybe you lacked communication, or perhaps you lost touch with your own identity. The pain helps you identify these areas so you can grow.

It Teaches You Resilience:

Breakups test your emotional limits, but they also show you what you're capable of enduring. Each day you get through is proof of your strength, even if it doesn't feel like it.

It Forces Growth:

Pain pushes you out of your comfort zone. It's uncomfortable, yes, but it's also where transformation happens. Use this time to evaluate what you want in your next relationship—or whether you even want one at all.

Who Are You Without Them? Rediscovering Your Identity

One of the hardest parts of healing isn't just getting over the person—it's getting over the version of yourself that existed in the relationship.

Breakups don't just take away a partner; they force you to confront who you are without them. If you were deeply invested in the relationship, it's possible you lost parts of yourself along the way—your hobbies, your routines, your dreams.

Ask Yourself:
- ✓ Who was I before this relationship?
- ✓ What did I love doing before I met them?
- ✓ What parts of myself did I sacrifice to make this relationship work?

Why This Matters
Many people cling to a past relationship because they feel like they lost a piece of themselves in it.

But here's the truth:
- ✓ You are still that person.
- ✓ Your identity is not tied to your ex.
- ✓ You don't need them to be whole again—you just need to reconnect with yourself.

Rebuilding Your Sense of Self
- ✓ Think back to the version of you that existed before the relationship.
- ✓ What activities made you feel alive, happy, and fulfilled?
- ✓ Make a conscious decision to reclaim those pieces of yourself.

Action Step: Reclaim Your Identity
Write down 5 things you loved doing before this relationship and commit to doing them again.
These can be small daily habits or big personal goals.

Examples:
- ✓ Reading books you love;
- ✓ Going to the gym or doing physical activities;
- ✓ Spending time with certain friends or family;
- ✓ Traveling, learning new skills, or pursuing creative hobbie;s
- ✓ Setting new personal or career goals.

☞ The goal: Reconnect with who you were before the relationship—and become an even stronger version of yourself.

Actionable Healing Strategies

Healing from a breakup is a process that requires intention, effort, and time. While the pain is inevitable, how you navigate it determines whether it will break you or build you. Below are expanded strategies to help you move through the pain with strength and purpose.

Create Space to Grieve

Healing starts with acknowledging the loss. Pretending you're fine or suppressing your emotions will only delay the process.

Steps to Grieve Intentionally:
Set Aside Time for Reflection:

Dedicate 10–15 minutes daily to sit with your feelings. Cry if you need to. Let the sadness, anger, or confusion surface without judgment.

Example: Sit in a quiet space, close your eyes, and let yourself feel whatever comes up. Journaling during this time can help release pent-up emotions.

Honor What Was Lost:
Acknowledge the good parts of the relationship while also recognizing why it ended. This balance prevents you from idealizing or demonizing the past.

Actionable Step: Write a letter to your ex (that you won't send), expressing gratitude for the good times and closure for the pain.

Allow for Ups and Downs:
Healing isn't linear. Some days, you'll feel strong; others, you'll feel like you've taken steps backward. This is normal—be patient with yourself.

Breakups often leave you feeling lost, especially if the relationship consumed a large part of your identity. Now is the time to rediscover who you are outside of the relationship.

Steps to Rebuild Your Identity:
Reflect on What You Love:
Make a list of activities, hobbies, or passions you enjoyed before the relationship. Start reintroducing them into your life.

Example: If you loved painting but gave it up during the relationship, buy some supplies and set aside time each week to create.

Explore New Interests, and use this time to try something you've always wanted to do. Learning new skills or pursuing fresh interests can give you a sense of excitement and purpose.

Actionable Step: Sign up for a cooking class, join a fitness group, or learn a new language

Rebuild Your Social Circle:
Reconnect with friends or family you may have distanced yourself from during the relationship. Surround yourself with people who uplift and support you.

Build Daily Routines for Stability
Breakups disrupt your sense of normalcy, so creating routines helps reestablish stability and structure in your life.

Steps to Establish a Healing Routine:
Morning Rituals:
Start your day with intention. Spend 5–10 minutes journaling about what you're grateful for or set goals for the day.

Example: Write, *"Today, I will focus on self-care by going for a walk and eating a healthy meal."*

Physical Activity:
Exercise isn't just good for your body—it boosts endorphins and helps you process emotions. Choose activities you enjoy, whether it's yoga, running, or dance.

Actionable Step: Commit to moving your body for 20–30 minutes a day. Even a brisk walk can make a difference.

Evening Wind-Down:
End your day with a calming activity like reading, meditating, or listening to soothing music. Avoid using screens before bed to give your mind time to rest.

Set Boundaries with Your Ex
Healing becomes difficult if you're constantly reopening wounds by staying overly connected to your ex.

Steps to Establish Healthy Boundaries:
- Limit Communication: Take a break from texting, calling, or checking their social media. This time apart allows you to focus on your own healing.
- Actionable Step: Consider unfollowing or muting your ex on social media to avoid triggering posts.
- Define Clear Boundaries: If you need to remain in contact (e.g., for co-parenting), set clear rules about when and how you'll communicate.
  Example: Agree to discuss logistics over email instead of emotional phone calls.

Resist the Urge to Seek Closure:
While it's tempting to reach out for *"one last conversation,"* this often prolongs the pain. Instead, focus on finding closure within yourself.

Reframe Negative Thoughts
Breakups often lead to spiraling thoughts of self-doubt, regret, or fear about the future. Reframing these thoughts helps you regain control over your mindset.

Steps to Reframe Negativity:

Challenge Your Inner Critic:
When you catch yourself thinking, *"I'll never find someone else,"* counter it with evidence to the contrary. *"This is a chance to focus on myself, and when the time is right, I'll find someone who values me."*

Focus on What You Can Control:
Shift your energy from what went wrong to what you can improve moving forward.

Actionable Step: Write down one lesson you learned from the relationship and how you'll apply it in the future.

Reinforce positive beliefs about yourself by repeating affirmations like, *"I am worthy of love and happiness,"* or *"This pain is temporary, and I'm growing stronger every day."*

Seek Support

Healing doesn't have to be a solo journey. Leaning on others can provide perspective, encouragement, and a sense of connection.

Steps to Build a Support System:
Talk to Trusted Friends or Family:

Share your feelings with people who will listen without judgment.

Example: Call a friend and say, *"I'm having a tough day. Can we talk for a bit?"*

Consider Professional Help:

A therapist or counselor can help you navigate the emotional complexities of a breakup and provide actionable tools for healing.

Join a Support Group:

Connecting with others who are going through similar experiences can make you feel less alone and offer valuable insights.

Focus on Future Goals

Shifting your attention to the future helps you move forward with purpose and hope.

Steps to Set Goals for the Future:

Revisit Old Dreams:

Think about goals you set aside during your relationship and start working toward them again.

Example: If you always wanted to start a side business, now is the time to take the first steps.

Set Short- and Long-Term Goals:

Break your goals into manageable steps to avoid feeling overwhelmed.

Actionable Step: Create a vision board to visualize what you want your life to look like in six months or a year.

Celebrate Small Wins:

Recognize and celebrate every step you take toward building a better life. This reinforces your progress and keeps you motivated.

When Healing Alone Isn't Enough: Knowing When to Seek Therapy

Breakups are painful, but for some people, they trigger deeper emotional wounds. If you're struggling to move forward, feeling constantly overwhelmed, or experiencing intense emotions that won't fade, it might be time to seek professional support.

💡 There's no shame in getting help. Therapy isn't a sign of weakness—it's a tool for gaining clarity, emotional stability, and a path forward.

Signs That You Might Need Professional Support

If you relate to multiple signs on this list, consider reaching out to a professional:

- ➢ You feel stuck in deep sadness that hasn't improved for months.
- ➢ You've lost interest in things you once enjoyed—hobbies, socializing, or self-care.
- ➢ You struggle to get out of bed or find motivation for daily life.
- ➢ You feel numb, hopeless, or disconnected from everything.
- ➢ You experience intense anxiety, panic attacks, or overwhelming emotions.
- ➢ You've developed unhealthy coping habits (drinking excessively, overeating, isolating yourself).
- ➢ You constantly replay the breakup in your head and feel unable to stop obsessing.
- ➢ You believe you'll never trust or love again.

💡 If you checked more than a few, don't ignore these signs—therapy could help you heal faster and more effectively.

How Therapy Helps You Heal Faster
Therapists can help you:

- ✓ Process the emotions you're struggling with.
- ✓ Identify patterns that led to the breakup and avoid repeating them.
- ✓ Rebuild confidence and self-worth.
- ✓ Develop healthy coping mechanisms to replace negative habits.
- ✓ Break free from past emotional trauma that's holding you back.

You don't have to do this alone. Seeking professional help isn't about being "broken"—it's about giving yourself the best chance to heal fully.

Action Step: Take Control of Your Emotional Well-Being
1. Ask yourself: Would I recommend therapy to a friend in my situation?
2. If the answer is yes, start researching therapists in your area or online.

Tough Love Reminder: Healing isn't about erasing the pain—it's about transforming it. The breakup is just one chapter in your story, not the entire book. By committing to these strategies and taking action every day, you'll emerge stronger, wiser, and ready for whatever comes next.

Discussion Questions:

1. What truth in this chapter hit you the hardest? Why?

2. Have you ever been in a relationship where the other person moved on faster than you expected? How did that impact you?

3. How do you typically process loss and rejection—do you shut down, seek distractions, or confront it head-on?

4. If closure isn't guaranteed, how can you create it for yourself?

5. What is one belief about love or relationships that this chapter made you question?

6. Looking back, were there moments where you felt your partner was already preparing to leave, but you ignored it?

7. How can you start focusing on yourself instead of waiting for answers from someone who has already left?

"The hardest truth to accept is that sometimes, no matter how much you want to, you can't fix what's already broken."

"Closure isn't something they give you—it's something you create for yourself."

"Letting go isn't about giving up. It's about choosing yourself."

CHAPTER 5
MONEY & BREAKUPS – THE FINANCIAL FALLOUT

The Financial Impact of Breakups (And How to Prepare)

Breakups don't just leave emotional scars—they can also take a serious financial toll. If you shared expenses, lived together, or relied on a joint financial system, the end of a relationship can feel like a financial earthquake. Some people stay in unhealthy relationships not because they love their partner, but because they fear financial instability more than emotional pain.

However, avoiding a breakup due to financial dependence can trap you in a cycle of stagnation and resentment. The truth is, you can recover emotionally and financially. But to do so, you need a solid plan.

The Hidden Costs of a Breakup

Splitting Assets – Who keeps what? Furniture, shared bank accounts, cars, pets, even gym memberships can become points of tension.

Housing Disruptions – If you lived together, one of you will likely have to move out, which means new rent, deposits, and living costs. If both names are on the lease or mortgage, this becomes even more complicated.

Income Adjustments – If your partner contributed financially, or vice versa, you may need to reassess your budget immediately. Losing a dual-income household can be a significant financial shock.

Legal Fees – If marriage, shared property, or child custody is involved, legal fees can pile up quickly. Even an amicable split can cost thousands in legal mediation, especially when dividing assets.

Debt Liability – Many couples co-sign loans, share credit cards, or take on joint debt, which means that after a breakup, one person could be left responsible for payments they didn't even make.

Emotional Spending – Many people make financially reckless choices during a breakup, such as retail therapy, spontaneous travel, eating out excessively, or even gambling.

Credit Score Damage – If your ex stops making payments on joint debts, shared accounts, or co-signed loans, your credit score could be affected—sometimes without you realizing it.

Breakups can set you back financially—unless you take control early.

How to Financially Prepare for a Breakup

If you're still in the early stages of separation, here's how to avoid financial disaster:

Step 1: Get Clear on Your Financial Picture

Track every expense. List all shared bills, subscriptions, rent/mortgage, and joint financial responsibilities. Know exactly how much you need to survive on your own.

Identify shared debts. Are you a co-signer on any loans? Do you have a joint credit card? If so, figure out a plan to separate financial obligations.

Assess your credit score. If you don't know your score, now is the time to check. Ensure no surprise charges appear from shared accounts.

Step 2: Separate Finances Immediately

Move any direct deposits or automatic payments into an individual account you control.

Close or separate joint accounts if possible. If closing is not an option, ensure you're not liable for your ex's spending.

Document any shared financial agreements in writing to prevent future legal disputes.

Step 3: Create an Emergency Fund

If you don't have savings, start setting aside money immediately to cover rent, legal fees, or unexpected expenses.

Even small amounts ($10-$20 per week) can make a huge difference if a financial emergency arises.

Step 4: Plan for Worst-Case Scenarios

If you need to move out, research affordable housing options.

If your ex was paying significant bills, create an emergency budget that cuts unnecessary costs.

If you were financially dependent, start looking at income options such as freelancing, side hustles, or upskilling to boost your earning potential.

Your financial freedom determines your emotional freedom. The sooner you take control, the faster you'll move forward.

Potential Bankruptcy After a Breakup

Some breakups leave people in financial ruin, especially when there are high debts, shared liabilities, or a drastic drop in income.

Warning Signs That You May Be Facing Bankruptcy After a Breakup:

If you are experiencing multiple financial setbacks after a breakup, you may be on the path toward bankruptcy without realizing it. Here are key warning signs that indicate the need for immediate action:

You can no longer afford rent or basic living expenses without financial assistance.

If you relied on a dual-income household and now struggle to cover essentials such as rent, groceries, and utilities, this is a major financial red flag.

You have significant joint debts that you are now responsible for.

Even if your ex was the one who spent the most on credit cards or loans, if your name is on those accounts, you are legally responsible for repayment.

You are maxing out credit cards just to survive.

If you find yourself relying on credit for everyday expenses, making only minimum payments, or borrowing money to stay afloat, this is a sign of financial instability.

Your ex stopped paying their share of joint bills, and creditors are now pursuing you.

Many people assume that if a bill was shared, both parties will continue making payments post-breakup. However, if your ex abandons their financial responsibility, debt collectors will come after you—even if you were not the one who incurred the debt.

Your credit score has dropped significantly due to missed payments.

A sudden drop in your credit score may indicate late payments, high credit utilization, or delinquent accounts, all of which can make it harder to get loans, rent an apartment, or even secure employment.

If any of these warning signs sound familiar, it is important to take action before the situation worsens.

What to Do If You're Facing Bankruptcy

If you are experiencing financial distress after a breakup, bankruptcy should be a last resort—but that does not mean ignoring your financial issues. Here is a step-by-step plan to help you regain control.

Step 1: Get Professional Advice

Speak to a Financial Advisor or Insolvency Trustee.

Before filing for bankruptcy, consult a licensed insolvency trustee or financial advisor. They can assess your full financial situation and help you understand:

Whether you qualify for debt relief programs

If you can negotiate your debts instead of filing for bankruptcy

The long-term impact of bankruptcy on your credit and future financial options

Step 2: **Contact Your Creditors and Negotiate Your Debt**

Many creditors would rather restructure your debt than have you declare bankruptcy. You may be able to:

Request lower interest rates or reduced monthly payments.

Negotiate a payment plan that works within your new financial reality.

Ask for temporary forbearance (a pause on payments) if you need time to recover.

Ignoring calls from creditors will only make the situation worse. Being proactive gives you a better chance of avoiding legal action.

Step 3: **Cut Unnecessary Expenses Immediately**

In a financial crisis, your spending needs to shift from *"nice-to-have"* to *"need-to-survive."*

Cancel any subscription services that are not essential, such as streaming services, gym memberships, or delivery apps.

Reduce discretionary spending on takeout, shopping, entertainment, and non-urgent travel.

Focus only on housing, food, and utilities while working through your financial plan.

Step 4: **Consider Debt Consolidation or a Consumer Proposal**

If your debt load is high but not completely unmanageable, there are alternatives to bankruptcy:

Debt Consolidation Loan – If you have multiple debts with high interest, consolidating them into one lower-interest loan can make payments more manageable.

Consumer Proposal – A consumer proposal allows you to negotiate a reduced amount of your debt without going bankrupt. It freezes interest, stops creditor harassment, and lets you pay back a portion of what you owe over a set period.

Debt Management Program (DMP) – In some cases, credit counseling agencies can help reduce your total debt and interest rates, making it easier to repay what you owe.

Step 5: If Bankruptcy Is the Only Option, Understand the Consequences

If bankruptcy is unavoidable, it is important to understand what it means for your financial future.

Your credit score will be severely impacted for up to seven years (or longer, depending on your country's bankruptcy laws).

You may have to surrender assets, such as vehicles or luxury items, depending on local laws.

Certain debts cannot be erased through bankruptcy, including student loans (in many cases), child support, and some tax debts.

It may be difficult to get approved for loans, mortgages, or rental applications after filing.

While bankruptcy can offer a fresh start, it is a serious financial decision that should only be considered after exploring all other options.

How to Recover Financially After Bankruptcy

If you have already declared bankruptcy, your financial future is not over—but you need a strategic plan to rebuild.

- ✓ Establish New Financial Habits
- ✓ Bankruptcy can be a wake-up call to develop better spending and saving habits.
- ✓ Create a strict budget and stick to it.
- ✓ Build an emergency fund, even if it is just a small amount per paycheck.
- ✓ Avoid taking on new debt unless absolutely necessary.
- ✓ Rebuild Your Credit Score

After bankruptcy, your credit score will be at its lowest point. Start rebuilding by:
- ✓ Applying for a secured credit card and making small, regular payments on time.
- ✓ Paying all bills before their due date to show responsible financial behavior.
- ✓ Keeping your credit utilization below 30 percent.
- ✓ Find New Income Streams

To regain financial independence, look for ways to increase your income:
- ✓ Start a side hustle or freelance work.
- ✓ Take on part-time jobs while searching for full-time opportunities.
- ✓ Learn a new skill or get certifications that increase your employability.
- ✓ Seek Professional Guidance for Financial Planning

Once you have stabilized, consider working with a financial planner to:
- ✓ Set long-term financial goals.
- ✓ Build a debt-free plan for the future.
- ✓ Invest wisely to create new wealth.

Act Now to Protect Your Future

If you are already in financial trouble, ignoring it will only make things worse. Whether you are on the verge of bankruptcy or just struggling to stay afloat, the best time to take action is now.

Key Takeaways:
Do not wait until debt collectors are at your door—be proactive.

Bankruptcy is not the only option—explore debt restructuring, consolidation, and consumer proposals first.

Rebuilding is possible, but it takes time, patience, and smart financial choices.

Breakups can feel like the end of the world—but financially speaking, they do not have to be. If you take control now, you will come out stronger, smarter, and more financially independent than ever before.

If You Were the Primary Earner and Now Feel Financially Drained

If you paid for most things in the relationship, you might feel:

- ✓ Like you *"wasted"* money on someone who didn't appreciate you.
- ✓ Frustrated that your ex is financially stable while you're struggling.
- ✓ Anxious about alimony, child support, or debt tied to the relationship.

How to Take Back Control
Separate emotions from money. You didn't *"lose"* money—you invested in an experience. Learn from it and move forward.

Cut unnecessary financial ties immediately. If your ex is still on your phone plan, car insurance, or credit card, remove them.

If legal action is involved, get professional advice. Don't assume anything—know your rights.

Your financial security should never depend on someone else. This is your chance to rebuild stronger than before.

If You Were Financially Dependent on Your Ex:
If your partner was the primary provider, you might feel:

- ✓ Like you're starting over with nothing.
- ✓ Afraid of how to support yourself alone.
- ✓ Pressured to find a new relationship just for financial security.

How to Take Back Control

- ✓ Secure your essentials first. Focus on covering rent, food, and bills before worrying about lifestyle changes.
- ✓ Get support. If necessary, explore financial aid programs, career development resources, or temporary side gigs to regain stability.
- ✓ Use this time to become financially independent. Whether it's learning a new skill, starting a small business, or investing wisely, use this as an opportunity to never be financially dependent again.

You are not powerless. You are rebuilding, one step at a time.

Create Your Post-Breakup Financial Plan

- ✓ Make a survival budget. How much do you need per month to live.
- ✓ List and cut unnecessary expenses. Avoid breakup-driven financial self-sabotage.
- ✓ Start saving, even a little. Every dollar saved is a step toward full independence.
- ✓ Seek financial or legal advice if necessary. Don't let confusion cost you more.

Discussion Questions:

1. What keeps people clinging to relationships even when they know deep down it's over?
2. What is your biggest fear about letting go of a relationship?
3. How do you personally define a healthy breakup? Is it even possible?
4. What emotional patterns do you notice in your past breakups?
5. Have you ever held onto hope for reconciliation when deep down, you knew it wouldn't happen?
6. If you knew for certain that your ex would never come back, how would that change your healing process?
7. What is one thing you need to do right now to fully accept and move forward?

"The pain is real, but so is your ability to heal."

"You don't move on by pretending it never happened. You move on by confronting it, processing it, and deciding it won't define you."

"Your next chapter doesn't start when someone else enters your life—it starts when you choose yourself."

CHAPTER 6
MEN VS. WOMEN: HOW WE PROCESS BREAKUPS DIFFERENTLY

Do Men and Women Handle Breakups Differently? A Psychological Perspective

Breakups impact both men and women, but extensive psychology research suggests they experience and process romantic loss in distinct and measurable ways. These differences are influenced by biological, psychological, and social factors, which shape how each gender reacts to the end of a relationship, copes with emotional pain, and ultimately heals.

Understanding these differences can help you navigate your own healing journey, recognize potential behavioral patterns, and avoid destructive post-breakup cycles.

How Women Handle Breakups: The Emotional First Responders

Research in relationship psychology indicates that women tend to process breakups more intensely but recover faster than men. A study published in Evolutionary Behavioral Sciences found that women experience more immediate emotional pain after a breakup, but they also engage in more adaptive coping strategies that help them heal over time.

Key Factors That Influence Women's Breakup Recovery:
Emotional Detachment Before the Breakup:
Studies suggest that women mentally leave relationships before they physically leave them. Research published in the Journal of Social and Personal Relationships found that women often initiate breakups because they have already emotionally disengaged, making it seem like they "move on faster."

Seeking Emotional Support Immediately:
Women tend to have stronger social networks, which play a crucial role in their healing process. According to research in Psychological Science, women rely on friends, family, and therapists to talk through their emotions, which significantly reduces long-term distress.

Allowing Themselves to Grieve:
Women are more likely to engage in open emotional processing, which involves fully experiencing their emotions rather than suppressing them. Studies show that expressing emotions rather than avoiding them leads to better long-term emotional regulation.

Focusing on Self-Improvement:

Post-breakup, many women prioritize self-care, including fitness, therapy, and personal development. This aligns with research in Emotion, which found that actively engaging in self-reflection and growth leads to faster emotional recovery.

For women, breakups are often about emotional closure and regaining self-worth. They may still feel pain, but their outlet for healing is immediate and socially accepted, helping them process emotions effectively.

How Men Handle Breakups: Delayed Emotional Fallout

Men tend to process breakups differently from women. While they may appear to recover quickly, research indicates that their grieving process is often delayed and can last much longer.

A study conducted by Binghamton University and University College London found that while women feel greater emotional pain immediately after a breakup, men report feeling more distress over time because they often fail to process their emotions effectively.

Key Factors That Influence Men's Breakup Recovery
Suppressing Rather Than Expressing Emotions:
Society conditions men to be emotionally self-reliant, discouraging them from discussing their pain. Research in Men and Masculinities found that many men internalize their emotions, leading to higher rates of depression and anxiety post-breakup.

Using Distraction Instead of Processing Pain:
Men often turn to work, casual relationships, alcohol, or excessive exercise as a way to avoid dealing with their emotions. A study in Clinical Psychological Science found that men engage in *"avoidant coping mechanisms"* at higher rates than women, which can lead to prolonged emotional distress.

Delayed Emotional Impact
Because men often suppress their emotions early on, they experience a delayed form of grief. This is why, months after a breakup, many men start feeling intense emotional pain—long after their ex has already moved on.

Struggling with Loneliness:

Men typically have fewer emotional support systems than women, which makes the healing process more difficult. A 2021 study in The Journal of Marriage and Family found that men are more likely to rely on their romantic partner as their primary source of emotional support, meaning that after a breakup, they often find themselves isolated and without guidance.

For men, breakups are often about losing a sense of stability, identity, and routine. The emotional impact may not be obvious at first, but if left unaddressed, it can lead to long-term emotional distress.

Why It Seems Like Women Move On Faster:

Many men assume that their ex *"moved on too fast,"* but psychological research suggests a different reality. The reason it appears that women heal faster is that they:

- ✓ Process emotions while still in the relationship: Women often detach emotionally before they physically leave, which means they start grieving the loss before the actual breakup;
- ✓ Seek immediate support: Women surround themselves with friends, family, and therapists, allowing them to release emotions faster rather than suppressing them;
- ✓ Engage in active healing strategies: Women intentionally focus on recovery, using self-care, therapy, and personal development to regain confidence.

Meanwhile, many men do not fully feel the loss until months later, when distractions fade, and they realize they never actually processed the breakup.

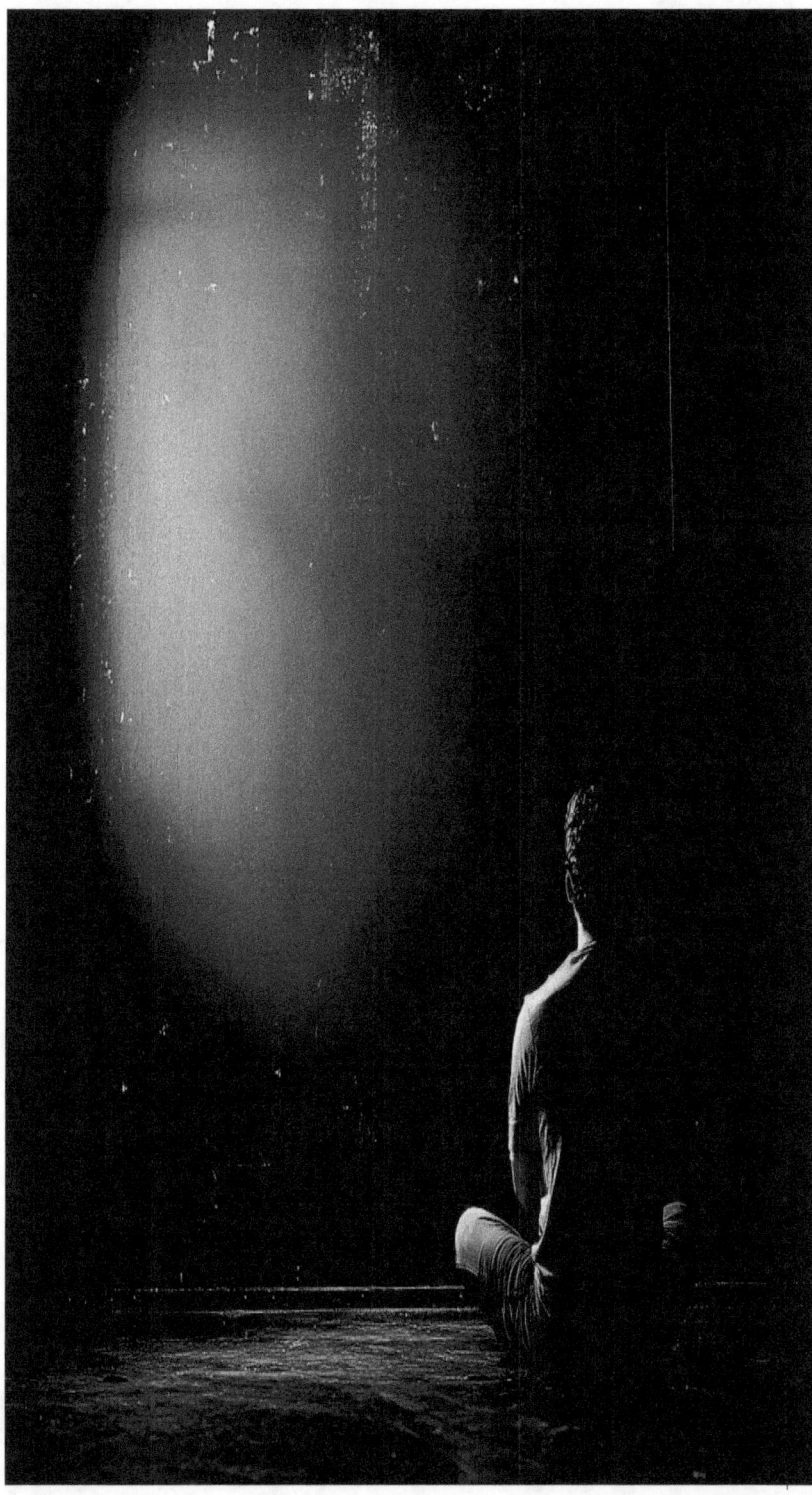

What Men Can Learn From Women (And Vice Versa)

Lessons Men Can Learn from Women:

Allow yourself to feel emotions instead of numbing them.

Suppressing pain does not eliminate it—it only postpones it. Processing emotions head-on leads to faster healing.

Seek support—whether through close friends, therapy, or a community.

Emotional resilience does not mean facing pain alone. Speaking to someone helps clarify feelings and speeds up recovery.

Prioritize healing through self-care rather than avoidance.

Instead of jumping into distractions, focus on personal growth, therapy, or self-improvement strategies.

Lessons Women Can Learn from Men

Avoid overanalyzing or obsessing over what went wrong.
Many women ruminate over breakups for too long, delaying closure. Letting go of "what could have been" allows faster emotional recovery.

Focus on action-based healing instead of just emotional processing.
While talking about feelings is important, taking real action—such as setting new goals or building a new routine—creates long-term healing.

Set boundaries early to prevent unnecessary emotional pain.
Recognizing toxic cycles and emotional over-investment early on prevents prolonged suffering.

Breakups are painful for everyone. But the people who heal best are those who actively process their emotions rather than suppressing them.

The Goal is Growth, Not Comparison: How to Transform Breakup Pain into Personal Power

One of the most destructive post-breakup habits is comparing yourself to your ex—how fast they moved on, how well they seem to be doing, or even whether they appear happier without you. This is a dangerous mindset because it traps you in a cycle of self-doubt, resentment, and emotional paralysis rather than helping you grow.

The truth is that breakups are not a competition. It does not matter whether men or women *"handle breakups better"*—what matters is how you choose to heal and rebuild your life.

Instead of focusing on whether your ex is ahead or behind in their healing journey, the real questions to ask yourself are:

Are you processing your emotions in a healthy way, or are you suppressing them?

Are you using this experience as an opportunity for self-reflection and growth?

Are you rebuilding your future with intention, or are you stuck dwelling on the past?

Every breakup, no matter how painful, holds an opportunity for transformation and self-discovery. The challenge is whether you will allow yourself to embrace that growth or stay stuck in bitterness and regret.

Why Comparison is the Biggest Threat to Your Healing

One of the greatest barriers to emotional recovery after a breakup is the comparison trap. You might find yourself:

- ✓ Obsessing over your ex's social media posts, trying to determine if they have moved on.
- ✓ Analyzing their dating life and feeling hurt if they seem to have found someone new.
- ✓ Questioning your worth based on how fast they *"recovered"* compared to you.
- ✓ Measuring your healing timeline against other people's, wondering why it is taking you longer.

The problem with comparison is that it keeps you emotionally tied to your past. Instead of using this breakup as an opportunity to grow, you are still mentally and emotionally invested in someone who is no longer in your life.

Research in cognitive psychology suggests that rumination—the tendency to repetitively think about past events—prolongs emotional distress and prevents individuals from moving forward. A study in the Journal of Personality and Social Psychology found that people who engage in social comparison after a breakup experience higher levels of depression and anxiety than those who focus on self-growth.

If you keep checking your ex's social media, wondering if they are happier without you, or mentally replaying conversations trying to figure out what went wrong, you are feeding the very emotions that are keeping you stuck.

How to Shift from Comparison to Growth

If you want to heal, rebuild, and emerge stronger, you must make a conscious decision to shift your focus from comparison to self-improvement. Here's how:

Stop Measuring Your Healing Against Theirs:

Your healing journey is yours alone. It is not dictated by how fast your ex moves on, how happy they look on Instagram, or what others expect from you.

Just because someone looks fine on the outside does not mean they are healed. External appearances can be deceiving. A study published in Cyberpsychology, Behavior, and Social Networking found that people frequently curate their social media to appear happier than they actually are, especially after a breakup.

Do not let their highlight reel disrupt your real healing.

Focus on Internal Reflection Instead of External Distractions

If you constantly check up on your ex or compare your progress to others, you are avoiding the deeper work that true healing requires. Instead of looking outward, ask yourself:

- ✓ What emotional patterns do I need to break?
- ✓ How did this relationship shape me, and what lessons can I take from it?
- ✓ What areas of my life have I been neglecting that I now have the opportunity to focus on?

The answers to these questions will do more for your healing than any comparison ever could.

Set Clear Goals for Your Post-Breakup Growth

Instead of measuring your healing by how quickly you feel better, measure it by your personal growth. Create tangible goals that reflect the version of yourself you are working toward.

Examples of post-breakup growth goals include:
- ✓ Emotional growth – Journaling, therapy, or self-reflection to break negative relationship patterns.
- ✓ Physical health – Exercising, improving your sleep, and eating healthier.
- ✓ Career or financial focus – Taking on new projects, learning new skills, or increasing your financial independence.
- ✓ New experiences – Traveling solo, trying a new hobby, or stepping outside your comfort zone.

By setting and pursuing these goals, you shift the focus away from your ex and back onto yourself, where it belongs.

Practice Gratitude for the Lessons You've Learned

It is easy to view a breakup as a failure or a loss, but the reality is that it is often a necessary redirection. Instead of being bitter about what ended, try shifting your mindset to what you gained from the experience.

Ask yourself:
- ✓ What did this relationship teach me about myself?
- ✓ How did this breakup expose areas where I need to grow?
- ✓ What qualities will I now look for in a future relationship that I never considered before?

By focusing on gratitude and growth, you reclaim the narrative of your breakup—not as something that broke you, but as something that built you into a stronger, wiser, and more self-aware person.

Your Breakup is Not the End—It is a New Beginning!

Many people treat breakups as a permanent emotional setback when, in reality, they are an opportunity for reinvention. You have two choices:

Stay stuck in comparison, resentment, and emotional stagnation.

Use this moment as a launchpad for your growth and transformation.

Growth does not mean pretending the pain does not exist—it means choosing to use that pain to fuel your progress. Instead of looking at your breakup as something that happened to you, look at it as something that happened to you.

If you embrace this experience as a catalyst for change, you will not just heal—you will become the version of yourself that is ready for a healthier, more fulfilling future.

The real question is: Will you allow yourself to grow, or will you stay stuck in the past?

Wake Up Before You Become the Statistic

This is not meant to scare you—it is meant to wake you up. The statistics are real. The consequences are real. But the good news is that you can take action before it is too late. You do not have to become part of the growing number of people who stay stuck in post-breakup depression for years.

The key to healing is not in who moves on faster, but in who chooses to actively work through their emotions and rebuild their life with purpose.

If you do the work now, you will not just recover—you will thrive.

Discussion Questions:

1. What has been your biggest roadblock in healing from past relationships?

2. How have your breakups shaped your self-worth and confidence?

3. What do you wish you had done differently in your last major breakup?

4. What is one unhealthy habit you tend to fall into after a breakup?

5. How do you personally handle loneliness after a relationship ends?

6. What would it look like to fully reclaim your happiness without depending on another person?

7. What is is one healing practice you can start implementing today?

"A breakup isn't the end of your story—it's the beginning of a new one."

"Your past relationship was a lesson, not a life sentence."

"The best revenge is not proving them wrong. It's proving to yourself that you were always enough."

CHAPTER 7
REBUILDING AFTER IT'S OVER

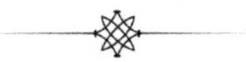

Introduction: A New Beginning
When the dust settle, and reconciliation is no longer an option, you're left with one choice: to rebuild. The end of a relationship can feel like the end of the world, but in reality, it's the beginning of a new chapter—one where you have the opportunity to redefine yourself, rediscover your passions, and create a future on your terms.

This chapter isn't about wallowing in what could have been. It's about action—taking deliberate steps to rebuild your self-worth, embrace your independence, and prepare for healthier, more fulfilling relationships in the future. If you've ever thought, *"How do I move forward from here?"* this is your guide.

Accepting That It's Over
Healing begins with acceptance. Fighting reality or holding onto false hope will only keep you stuck. Letting go doesn't mean giving up—it means freeing yourself to move forward.

Steps to Accept the End:
Release the Fantasy:
Let go of the *"perfect version"* of your relationship that exists in your mind. Acknowledge the reality of what the relationship was, including its flaws.

Example: Instead of saying, *"We were so happy; how did this happen?"* reframe it as, *"There were moments of happiness, but there were also significant issues we couldn't resolve."*

Create a Ritual for Closure:
Symbolic acts can help you emotionally let go.

Actionable Step: Write down everything you want to let go of—pain, regrets, unspoken words—and then safely burn the paper as a way to release it.

Avoid the *"What-If"* Spiral:
Questioning every decision or imagining alternate outcomes will keep you stuck in the past. Instead, focus on what's ahead.

Tough Love Reminder: You can't change the past, but you can shape your future.

Building Self-Worth:
After a breakup, it's common to feel like your sense of worth has been shattered. Rebuilding self-worth isn't just about feeling confident again—it's about recognizing your inherent value, independent of any relationship.

Steps to Rebuild Self-Worth:
Practice Daily Affirmations:
Reprogram negative thoughts by reinforcing positive beliefs about yourself.

Example: Repeat affirmations like, *"I am worthy of love and respect,"* or *"My value is not defined by my relationship status."*

Reflect on Your Strengths:
List qualities that make you unique—your kindness, resilience, humor—and remind yourself of the value you bring to the world.

Actionable Step: Keep a *"Strengths Journal"* where you write down one positive trait or accomplishment every day.

Focus on Self-Care:
Prioritize activities that nourish your body, mind, and soul.

Example: Commit to a regular fitness routine, try mindfulness meditation, or explore a creative hobby like painting or writing.

Celebrate Small Wins:
Every step forward—no matter how small—is progress. Acknowledge and celebrate these milestones to build momentum.

Example: Celebrate the first day you go without checking your ex's social media or the first time you feel genuinely happy again.

Rediscovering Your Identity
Breakups often leave you feeling like you've lost a part of yourself. This is the time to reconnect with who you are outside of the relationship.

Steps to Rediscover Your Identity:
Reconnect with Old Passions:
Think about hobbies, interests, or dreams you set aside during the relationship. Now is the time to revisit them.

Example: If you loved traveling but stopped during the relationship, plan a solo trip or explore nearby attractions.

Try New Experiences:
Growth happens when you step out of your comfort zone. Trying new activities can help you discover parts of yourself you didn't know existed.

Actionable Step: Join a local class or group—whether it's pottery, hiking, or a book club—and meet people who share your interests.

Set Personal Goals:
Focus on building a life that excites you. Whether it's advancing in your career, improving your health, or learning a new skill, setting goals gives you purpose.

Example: Create a vision board with images and words that represent the life you want to build.

Preparing for Healthier Relationships
Once you've rebuilt your foundation, it's natural to think about future relationships. But before jumping into something new, take the time to reflect on what you want and need in a partner.

Steps to Prepare for Future Relationships:

Identify Your Non-Negotiables:
Reflect on what worked and didn't work in your past relationship. Use these lessons to define your boundaries and deal-breakers.

Example: If lack of communication was a major issue, prioritize open dialogue in your next relationship.

Learn to Love Yourself First:
The healthiest relationships come from a place of self-love and independence. Make sure you're whole on your own before seeking a connection with someone else.

Tough Love Reminder: A partner should complement your life, not complete it.

Take It Slow:
Avoid rushing into a new relationship as a way to fill the void. Take the time to truly know yourself and the other person before committing.

Actionable Step: Practice intentional dating—focus on quality over quantity and evaluate whether a potential partner aligns with your values.

Communicate with Clarity:
Healthy relationships are built on honesty and transparency. Learn to express your needs, expectations, and feelings openly from the start.

Example: If you value quality time, communicate that to your partner early on rather than expecting them to *"figure it out."*

Embracing Your Independence:
Independence isn't just about being single—it's about knowing you can thrive on your own. Embracing your independence is the ultimate step in rebuilding after a breakup.

Steps to Embrace Independence:
Find Joy in Solitude:
Learn to enjoy your own company. Spend time doing activities you love without relying on others for validation.

Actionable Step: Schedule a solo *"date"* once a week—go to a coffee shop, watch a movie, or visit a museum.

Create a Supportive Environment:
Surround yourself with people, spaces, and routines that uplift you. Let go of toxic relationships or environments that drain your energy.

Example: Redecorate your space to reflect your style and make it a place where you feel at peace.

Focus on Your Personal Mission:
What legacy do you want to leave behind? Whether it's through your career, community involvement, or creative pursuits, channel your energy into something meaningful.

Example: Volunteer for a cause you're passionate about or start a side project that excites you.

Actionable Steps for Identity Rebuilding
Rediscovering your identity after a breakup is a transformative process. It's about reconnecting with who you are outside of the relationship, exploring new possibilities, and rebuilding a life that feels

authentic and fulfilling. Here's a detailed roadmap to help you rebuild your identity step by step.

Reflect on Who You Were Before the Relationship:
Relationships often shape our identities, but they can also cause us to lose touch with parts of ourselves. Start by revisiting who you were before your relationship began.

Steps to Reflect:
Write Down Your Pre-Relationship Passions:
List activities, hobbies, or interests you loved before the relationship. Did you enjoy painting, playing sports, traveling, or writing?

Example: *"Before the relationship, I loved hiking every weekend. I stopped because my partner wasn't interested."*

Recall Your Goals and Dreams:
Think about the aspirations you had before the relationship. Did you want to pursue a certain career, learn a new skill, or live in a specific city?

Actionable Step: Identify one goal or dream you still feel excited about and make a plan to pursue it.

Identify What You Gained and Lost in the Relationship:
Understanding how the relationship influenced you—both positively and negatively—can help you rebuild your sense of self with clarity.

Steps to Identify Gains and Losses:
Create a "Gains and Losses" Chart:
Divide a page into two columns. On one side, write what you gained from the relationship (e.g., new skills, perspectives, or experiences).

On the other, write what you lost (e.g., time for yourself, confidence, or friendships).

Focus on the Lessons Learned:
Reflect on how the relationship helped you grow, even if it ended.

Example: *"I learned how to communicate better and the importance of setting boundaries."*

Decide What to Reclaim:
Identify aspects of yourself you want to restore or strengthen.

Actionable Step: If you lost confidence during the relationship, take steps to rebuild it by trying something challenging or seeking professional development opportunities.

Reconnect with Old Passions and Hobbies
Rediscovering activities you once loved is a powerful way to reconnect with your authentic self.

Steps to Reconnect:
Make a "Passion Bucket List":
Write down 5–10 activities or hobbies you enjoyed before the relationship but set aside. Commit to reintroducing at least one of them into your life.

Example: *"I used to love playing guitar. I'll dedicate 30 minutes twice a week to practice."*

Revisit Old Spaces:
Go back to places or communities that were meaningful to you before the relationship, such as a favorite coffee shop, a gym, or a creative class.

Actionable Step: Join a local group or workshop related to your hobby to meet like-minded people.

Explore New Interests:

Breakups are an opportunity to redefine yourself and try things you've never done before.

Steps to Explore New Interests:
Experiment with Something Outside Your Comfort Zone:

Trying new activities can open up parts of yourself you didn't know existed.

Example: Take a dance class, sign up for a public speaking course, or learn a new language.

Set a Monthly Exploration Goal:

Each month, commit to trying one new experience. It doesn't have to be life-changing—it's about discovery.

Actionable Step: Attend a community event, try a new sport, or take a weekend trip to a nearby town.

Reassess Your Values and Priorities

Breakups give you the space to redefine what truly matters to you. Use this time to align your life with your core values.

Steps to Reassess:
Write Down Your Core Values:

Reflect on what's most important to you—family, creativity, independence, faith, health, etc.

Example: *"I value adventure, but I haven't prioritized it. I'll plan a solo trip this year."*

Evaluate How You Spent Your Time:
Look at how your time was divided during the relationship. Were you prioritizing things that mattered to you, or were you compromising too much?

Actionable Step: Realign your schedule to include activities and goals that reflect your values.

Create a Vision Statement:
Write a short statement about the life you want to build.

Example: *"I want to be someone who embraces creativity, prioritizes health, and lives with purpose."*

Rebuild Your Social Circle
Reconnecting with friends and meeting new people helps you rebuild your sense of belonging and community.

Steps to Rebuild Connections:
Reconnect with Old Friends:
Reach out to friends you may have drifted apart from during the relationship.

Actionable Step: Send a simple message like, *"Hey, I was thinking about you and wanted to catch up. Let's grab coffee soon."*

Expand Your Network:
Join clubs, attend meetups, or take part in community events to meet new people.

Example: Look for local groups on platforms like Meetup or Facebook that align with your interests.

Set Healthy Boundaries:
Ensure your social interactions are uplifting. Distance yourself from anyone who drains your energy or brings negativity.

Focus on Your Physical and Mental Health
Taking care of your body and mind is essential for rebuilding your sense of self.

Steps to Prioritize Health:
Create a Fitness Routine:
Physical activity improves mood, boosts energy, and builds confidence.

Actionable Step: Commit to exercising 3–4 times a week, whether it's walking, yoga, or strength training.

Practice Mindfulness:
Mindfulness helps you stay present and reduce anxiety about the future.

Example: Try guided meditations on apps like Headspace or Calm for 10 minutes daily.

Seek Therapy if Needed:
Professional guidance can help you navigate the emotional aftermath of a breakup and develop healthier habits.

Set Personal Goals and Track Progress
Setting goals gives you a sense of purpose and direction as you rebuild your identity.

Steps to Set Goals:
Start Small:
Break larger goals into smaller, achievable steps.

Example: If your goal is to write a book, start by committing to 500 words a week.

Track Your Achievements:
Keep a journal or digital tracker to record your progress and celebrate milestones.

Actionable Step: Reflect weekly on what you've accomplished and what you'll focus on next.

Discussion Questions:

1. What is your biggest takeaway from reading this book?
2. How has your perspective on relationships changed?
3. What is one lesson from your past relationships that will help you build a better future?
4. What patterns or habits do you want to break before entering your next relationship?
5. If you could give your past self advice before your last breakup, what would it be?
6. What are three non-negotiables you will set for your next relationship?
7. How will you know when you're truly ready to love again?

Rediscovering your identity after a breakup isn't about returning to who you were before—it's about building a stronger, wiser, and more authentic version of yourself. Embrace this journey with courage and curiosity, knowing that every step you take brings you closer to the life you deserve.

CONCLUSION: TURNING PAIN INTO POWER

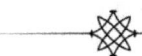

Breakups are never easy. They can feel like the ground beneath you has crumbled, leaving you lost, hurt, and questioning everything you thought you knew about love, life, and yourself. But here's the truth: what feels like the end of your world today is not the end of your story. It's the beginning of a new chapter—one where you have the power to redefine who you are, what you want, and how you live.

The pain you've experienced doesn't have to define you. Instead, it can serve as the foundation for something greater: growth, resilience, and a life that feels authentically yours. This book has been a journey through the tough truths, the uncomfortable realities, and the hard work of healing. But it's also been a journey of rediscovery—of your worth, your strength, and your ability to thrive, no matter what life throws at you.

The Lessons You've Learned

Throughout this book, you've explored the subtle signs of a failing relationship, the importance of taking responsibility, and the shocking realities of how relationships unravel. You've faced the emotional fallout of a breakup head-on, learning how to grieve without getting stuck in the pain. You've navigated the financial challenges that often accompany the end of a relationship, and you've gained insights into how men and women process breakups differently.

But more than that, you've taken the time to rebuild. You've rediscovered your identity, reconnected with your passions, and redefined what it means to love yourself. You've set boundaries, embraced your independence, and prepared for healthier, more fulfilling relationships in the future. These steps aren't just about healing—they're about transformation.

The Power of Choice

One of the most important lessons from this book is the power of choice. You can't control everything that happens to you, but you can control how you respond. You can choose to stay stuck in the pain, replaying the past and wondering what went wrong. Or you can choose to use that pain as fuel—to grow, to learn, and to create a life that feels meaningful and authentic.

Every choice you make from this moment forward is an opportunity to take back your power. Whether it's setting a new goal, trying something you've always wanted to do, or simply choosing to be kind to yourself on a hard day, these small actions add up to something extraordinary. They prove to yourself—and to the world—that you are not defined by your past, but by the courage and resilience you show in moving forward.

The Journey Ahead

Healing is not a straight line. There will be days when you feel strong, confident, and ready to take on the world. And there will be days when the pain feels fresh, when the memories come flooding back, and when you wonder if you'll ever truly move on. That's okay. Healing is a process, and it's okay to take it one step at a time.

What matters is that you keep moving forward. Even on the hard days, even when it feels like you're taking two steps back, remember that you're still moving. Every tear, every moment of reflection, every small act of self-care is a step toward a brighter future.

Your New Beginning

This breakup is not the end of your story. It's the start of a new chapter—one where you are the author. You get to decide what happens next. You get to decide who you want to be, what you want to do, and how you want to live.

Maybe this new chapter includes a new relationship, one built on the lessons you've learned and the boundaries you've set. Maybe it's a chapter of independence, where you focus on your career, your passions, and your personal growth. Or maybe it's a chapter of exploration, where you try new things, meet new people, and discover parts of yourself you never knew existed.

Whatever this new chapter looks like, know that you are ready for it. You've done the hard work. You've faced the tough truths. You've rebuilt yourself from the inside out. And now, you're stronger, wiser, and more resilient than ever before.

A Final Word of Encouragement

You are capable of more than you realize. The breakup may have knocked you down, but it hasn't broken you. By taking the actionable steps outlined in this book, you've proven to yourself—and to the world—that you are strong, worthy, and ready for whatever comes next.

So, take a deep breath. Look in the mirror and remind yourself of how far you've come. You've turned pain into power, and now it's time to step into the life you deserve.

The best is yet to come.

Call to Action: Your Next Steps

It's time to put what you've learned into action. Healing doesn't happen overnight, but every small step you take today will bring you closer to the life you deserve. Here's how to move forward:

Take Responsibility:
Revisit the lessons from this book and identify one key area where you can take ownership of your growth.

Actionable Step: Write down one habit or behavior you're committed to improving.

Set Your Intentions:
Decide what you want your next chapter to look like. Focus on building a life that excites and fulfills you.

Actionable Step: Create a vision board or journal about your ideal future.

Join a Community:
Surround yourself with people who inspire and uplift you. Healing is easier when you're supported.

Actionable Step: Find a local group, online forum, or support network where you can share your journey.

Keep Moving Forward:
Healing is a journey, not a destination. Celebrate your progress, no matter how small, and keep striving for growth.

Actionable Step: Reflect weekly on one win and one area you want to focus on.

Steps for Cultivating Self-Love After a Breakup
Self-love is the cornerstone of healing after a breakup. It's about treating yourself with kindness, rebuilding your confidence, and recognizing your worth independent of anyone else. Here's a step-by-step guide to rediscovering and nurturing self-love after a breakup.

Acknowledge Your Pain
Healing begins with acknowledging the pain and accepting that it's okay to feel hurt. Self-love isn't about ignoring your emotions; it's about giving yourself permission to process them.

Actionable Steps:
Name Your Feelings:
Write down exactly what you're feeling—sadness, anger, regret, relief—and validate those emotions without judgment.

Example: *"I feel angry because I gave so much of myself. It's okay to feel this way."*

Allow Yourself to Grieve:
Set aside time to cry, reflect, or even scream into a pillow if that's what you need. Suppressing emotions only prolongs the healing process.

Tough Love Reminder: Feeling your emotions is not a sign of weakness; it's a sign of courage.

Forgive Yourself
Breakups often come with a sense of guilt or self-blame. Self-love requires letting go of those feelings and forgiving yourself for mistakes you may have made.

Actionable Steps:
Write a Self-Forgiveness Letter:
Write a letter to yourself acknowledging any regrets and offering forgiveness.

Example: *"I forgive myself for not always communicating my needs clearly. I am learning and growing."*

Shift the Narrative:
Reframe negative thoughts with affirmations.
Example: Instead of saying, *"I failed at this relationship,"* say, *"I did my best with the tools I had, and now I'm learning to do better."*

Reconnect with Your Body
A breakup can leave you feeling disconnected from yourself. Rebuilding self-love starts with reconnecting with your physical self.

Actionable Steps:
Prioritize Movement:
Engage in activities that make you feel good in your body, like yoga, dancing, or walking. Physical activity releases endorphins and helps reduce stress.

Example: Sign up for a beginner's yoga class or take a daily 20-minute walk in nature.

Practice Mindful Self-Care:
Treat your body with love by indulging in nurturing routines like skincare, baths, or massage.

Actionable Step: Set aside one evening a week for a *"self-care night"* where you pamper yourself.

Explore Your Sensuality:

Reconnect with your body by wearing clothes that make you feel confident, experimenting with new hairstyles, or simply appreciating your physical presence.

Speak to Yourself with Kindness
Negative self-talk often peaks after a breakup, but it's one of the biggest barriers to self-love. Change the way you speak to yourself to foster confidence and compassion.

Actionable Steps:
Use Affirmations Daily:
Repeat affirmations like, *"I am enough,"* or *"I deserve love and respect."* Write them on sticky notes and place them around your home.

Reframe Negative Thoughts:

When you catch yourself thinking, *"I'm not good enough,"* challenge it by asking, *"What evidence do I have that this is true?"* Then, replace it with a positive truth.

Example: *"I'm not perfect, but I am worthy of love."*

Journal About Wins:
Write down one thing you like about yourself every day to shift your focus to your strengths.

Rediscover What Brings You Joy
Breakups create space to rediscover your passions and embrace what makes you happy.

Actionable Steps:
Create a Joy List:
Write a list of activities, places, or things that bring you joy. Make it a goal to incorporate at least one of them into your week.

Example: *"Reading by the window with a cup of tea"* or *"Dancing to my favorite songs in my living room."*

Try Something New:
Explore hobbies or experiences you've always wanted to try. Novelty can reignite your zest for life.

Actionable Step: Sign up for a painting class, join a local hiking group, or try cooking a new cuisine.

Set Healthy Boundaries
Self-love involves protecting your energy and setting boundaries that honor your needs.

Actionable Steps:
Say *"No"* Without Guilt:
Practice saying no to things that drain you or don't align with your values.

Example: Decline an invitation to events where you might feel pressured to explain your breakup.

Limit Interactions with Your Ex:
Establish boundaries for communication or distance if interacting with your ex hinders your healing.

Actionable Step: Mute or unfollow them on social media to avoid triggering posts.

Surround Yourself with Positivity:
Spend time with people who uplift and support you, and distance yourself from toxic or draining relationships.

Focus on Personal Growth
Self-love flourishes when you invest in your personal development and growth.

Actionable Steps:
Set Goals for Yourself:
Choose goals that excite you and help you build confidence.

Example: *"I want to learn how to swim by summer"* or *"I'll save money for a solo trip."*

Invest in Learning:
Read books, take courses, or attend workshops that align with your interests and aspirations.

Actionable Step: Enroll in an online course about something you've always been curious about, like photography or financial planning.

Reflect on Your Journey:
Regularly journal about how far you've come since the breakup and the lessons you've learned.

Create a Vision for Your Future
Visualizing the life you want builds hope and motivation, both of which are essential for self-love.

Actionable Steps:
Create a Vision Board:
Use images, words, and symbols that represent your ideal future—career goals, personal achievements, or new adventures.

Set Short- and Long-Term Goals:
Write down what you want to accomplish in the next six months, year, and beyond. Break these goals into manageable steps.

Example: If your goal is to improve your fitness, start by committing to three workouts a week.

Celebrate Milestones:
Acknowledge and reward yourself for progress, no matter how small. Self-love grows when you recognize your efforts.

Tough Love Reminder: Self-love is a practice, not a destination. It's about showing up for yourself every single day, even when it's hard. The breakup doesn't define you—how you rebuild and care for yourself does. This journey is yours to own, and you are worth every ounce of effort it takes.

The fact that you've made it this far means you're ready to turn your pain into power. This book is just the beginning. The real transformation happens when you commit to showing up for yourself every single day. Whether you're rebuilding your identity, preparing for healthier relationships, or simply learning to love your own company, remember: you are worthy, you are enough, and you are capable of creating a beautiful life beyond this breakup.

RESOURCES FOR FURTHER HEALING

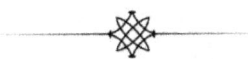

Healing after a breakup or divorce is a journey, and you don't have to do it alone. Below is a curated list of resources to help you navigate the emotional, financial, and spiritual aspects of recovery. Whether you're looking for therapy, financial planning tools, or faith-based support, these resources can provide guidance and encouragement as you move forward.

Celebrate Recovery
A Christ-centered recovery program for anyone struggling with hurt, pain, or addiction. It's a safe place to find community and healing.

Website: www.celebraterecovery.com

Resources by Country
Canada:
Canadian Mental Health Association (CMHA)
Offers mental health support and resources, including counseling and crisis intervention.
Website: www.cmha.ca

Credit Canada
Provides free credit counseling and debt management services.
Website: www.creditcanada.com

United States:
National Domestic Violence Hotline
Offers support for individuals experiencing abuse or control in their relationships.
Hotline: 1-800-799-SAFE (7233)
Website: www.thehotline.org
National Suicide Prevention Lifeline
Provides 24/7 support for anyone in emotional distress or crisis.
Hotline: 1-800-273-TALK (8255)
Website: www.suicidepreventionlifeline.org

United Kingdom:
Relate
Offers relationship counseling, divorce support, and family therapy services.
Website: www.relate.org.uk
StepChange Debt Charity
Provides free debt advice and support for individuals struggling with financial challenges.
Website: www.stepchange.org

4. **National Domestic Violence Hotline (U.S.)** – www.thehotline.org

   Support for individuals experiencing abuse or control in their relationships.

5. **Psychology Today Therapist Directory** – www.psychologytoday.com

   A comprehensive directory for finding relationship counselors and therapists near you.

Financial & Legal Resources

1. **National Foundation for Credit Counseling (NFCC)** – www.nfcc.org

   A non-profit offering free or low-cost financial counseling and debt management services.

2. **StepChange Debt Charity (UK)** – www.stepchange.org

   Free debt advice and support for individuals struggling with financial challenges.

3. **Credit Canada** – www.creditcanada.com

   Provides free credit counseling and debt management services in Canada.

4. **Mint (Budgeting App)** – www.mint.com

   A free app that helps track spending, create budgets, and manage finances.

5. **YNAB (You Need A Budget)** – www.ynab.com

   A budgeting tool to help manage finances and plan for the future.

FINAL NOTE

Healing is a journey, and it's okay to ask for help along the way. Whether you're seeking emotional support, financial guidance, or spiritual encouragement, these resources are here to help you take the next step toward a brighter future. Remember, you are not alone, and there is hope for a life filled with joy, purpose, and love—starting with yourself.

ABOUT THE AUTHOR

Sandro Ferreira is a keynote speaker, certified coach, and advocate for trauma-informed financial literacy. As an executive public speaker and entrepreneur, he has spent years helping people overcome barriers, shift their mindsets, and rebuild their lives with purpose.

After experiencing the pain of a breakup, Sandro dedicated himself to understanding the complexities of relationships, emotional resilience, and personal growth. He knows firsthand what it feels like to pour everything into a relationship—only to watch it unravel before his eyes. His journey from heartbreak to healing has fueled his mission: to help others recognize the warning signs, take control of their lives, and make empowered decisions about love, commitment, and self-worth.

Sandro's background in coaching, wealth-building, and leadership gives him a unique perspective on relationships, blending practical wisdom with tough love to help people break free from cycles of denial and take action before it's too late. He believes that while success in business is intentional, success in relationships requires the same level of awareness, effort, and strategy.

www.ingramcontent.com/pod-product-compliance
Lightning Source LLC
LaVergne TN
LVHW051603070426
835507LV00021B/2748